Substance Use Problems

About the Authors

Mitch Earleywine, PhD, is Associate Professor of Clinical Psychology at the University at Albany, State University of New York, where he teaches drugs and human behavior, substance abuse treatment and clinical research methods. He has received 10 teaching commendations, including the coveted General Education Teaching Award from the University of Southern California. His research funding has come from the National Institute on Alcohol Abuse and Alcoholism, the Alcoholic Beverage Medical Research Foundation, and the Marijuana Policy Project. He serves on the editorial boards of four psychology journals, reviews for over a dozen, and has more than 80 publications on drug use and abuse, including "Understanding Marijuana" (Oxford University Press, 2002). He serves on the advisory board for the National Organization for the Reform of Marijuana Laws, and is a member of the Research Society on Alcoholism, the Association for the Advancement of Behavior Therapy, and the Drug Policy Alliance.

Advances in Psychotherapy – Evidence-Based Practice

Danny Wedding; PhD, MPH, Prof., St. Louis, MO
(Series Editor)
Larry Beutler; PhD, Prof., Palo Alto, CA
Kenneth E. Freedland; PhD, Prof., St. Louis, MO
Linda C. Sobell; PhD, ABPP, Prof., Ft. Lauderdale, FL
David A. Wolfe; PhD, Prof., Toronto
(Associate Editors)

The basic objective of this series is to provide therapists with practical, evidence-based treatment guidance for the most common disorders seen in clinical practice – and to do so in a "reader-friendly" manner. Each book in the series is both a compact "how-to-do" reference on a particular disorder for use by professional clinicians in their daily work, as well as an ideal educational resource for students and for practice-oriented continuing education.

The most important feature of the books is that they are practical and "reader-friendly:" All are structured similarly and all provide a compact and easy-to-follow guide to all aspects that are relevant in real-life practice. Tables, boxed clinical "pearls", marginal notes, and summary boxes assist orientation, while checklists provide tools for use in daily practice.

Substance Use Problems

Mitch Earleywine
Clinical Psychology Department, University at Albany,
State University of New York

HOGREFE

Library of Congress Cataloging in Publication

is available via the Library of Congress Marc Database under the
LC Control Number 2009925364

Library and Archives Canada Cataloguing in Publication

Earleywine, Mitch
    Substance use problems / Mitch Earleywine.

(Advances in psychotherapy--evidence-based practice)
Includes bibliographical references.
ISBN 978-0-88937-329-7

    1. Drug abuse. 2. Drug abuse--Treatment. I. Title. II. Series: Advances in
psychotherapy--evidence-based practice

RC564.E25 2009   616.86'0651   C2009-901894-2

PUBLISHING OFFICES
USA: Hogrefe Publishing, 875 Massachusetts Avenue, 7th Floor,
                Cambridge, MA 02139
                Phone (866) 823-4726, Fax (617) 354-6875; E-mail info@hogrefe.com
EUROPE: Hogrefe & Huber Publishers, Rohnsweg 25, 37085 Göttingen, Germany
                Phone +49 551 49609-0, Fax +49 551 49609-88, E-mail hh@hogrefe.com

SALES & DISTRIBUTION
USA: Hogrefe Publishing, Customer Services Department,
                30 Amberwood Parkway, Ashland, OH 44805
                Phone (800) 228-3749, Fax (419) 281-6883, E-mail custserv@hogrefe.com
EUROPE: Hogrefe & Huber Publishers, Rohnsweg 25, 37085 Göttingen, Germany
                Phone +49 551 49609-0, Fax +49 551 49609-88, E-mail hh@hogrefe.com

OTHER OFFICES
CANADA: Hogrefe & Huber Publishers, 1543 Bayview Avenue, Toronto, Ontario M4G 3B5
SWITZERLAND: Hogrefe & Huber Publishers, Länggass-Strasse 76, CH-3000 Bern 9

Hogrefe & Huber Publishers
Incorporated and registered in Göttingen, Lower Saxony, Germany

Hogrefe Publishing
Incorporated and registered in the Commonwealth of Massachusetts, USA

Printed and bound in the USA
ISBN 978-0-88937-329-7

Acknowledgments

My hearty thanks to Danny Wedding, Robert Dimbleby, and Linda Sobell for keeping me involved in this project. I thank my clinical supervisees who encouraged me to elaborate on these points. The graduate students who took the substance abuse treatment course in the last 17 years deserve congratulations for keeping me on top of this literature while encouraging me to explain it efficiently. The thousands (!) who took the infamous "Drug Class" kept me excited about these topics by letting me see this field through their eyes. My usual support team also gets unusual kudos: Robert Earleywine, Clark and Suzy Van Scoyk, David and Felice Gordis, Joe Earleywine (who critiqued sections with great candor and minimal ridicule), Jack Huntington, Rob Kampia, Bruce Mirken, Paul Armentano, Allen St. Pierre, Keith Stroup, Marsha Rosenbaum, Ethan Nadelmann, Stanton Peele, and Domenico Scarlatti. My unbridled thanks to Nicholas Van Dam, who deserves an award for reading every word of this document and many that didn't make it. His comments improved the book dramatically. Special thanks to Michelle Stiles, who turned my free associations into references. I also thank my new support team: The Musketeers (Brad Armour-Garb, Tony DeBlasi, and Larry Kranich), Mike and Valerie Corral, Wendy Chapkis, and Russ Belville. Jenny Rella, Justina Farley, and Bryan O'Neill also get my sincere gratitude.

My daughters, Dahlia and Maya, continue to teach me that no matter how much I may know about genetics and environment, I cannot explain all the variance in behavior. My wife, Elana, continues to show inexplicable support, including astounding clinical skill at dealing with frequent and severe bouts of DMS (drug manuscript syndrome). I dedicate this book to her with love.

But I think I owe the biggest debt to the clients who sat with me as we all crawled, walked, ran, and occasionally flew toward better lives.

Table of Contents

1

Description of Problem Drug Use

1.1   Terminology

This first section reviews diagnostic terms, epidemiology, prognosis, differential diagnosis, comorbidities, and diagnostic procedures for drug-related problems. A clear understanding of each of these topics will lay a foundation for efficient assessment and treatment.

1.1.1   Diagnostic Terms

Defining problem drug use can seem like a fool's errand. Some people clearly have their lives altered by their use of psychoactive substances; others seem to use without troubles. The range of substances, intoxication experiences, and negative consequences is vast. Several terms appear to describe drug problems adequately, but many others are imprecise, ambiguous, or pejorative. The definition of problematic use reflects tacit assumptions about drugs and drug users. These assumptions can alter our interactions with clients in ways that may escape our awareness. Those who consider illicit drug use (or any illegal behavior) inherently wrong can find that their interactions with these clients differ dramatically from their interactions with other clients. The moral implications of using drugs change in different environments and different eras. Perhaps the best perspective for defining problem drug use requires understanding the goal of the definition. Ideally, identifying drug problems could serve as a step toward building a productive therapeutic relationship. Precise names for these problems can also aid communication within a treatment team. When everyone involved gives the same meaning to terms like dependence, abuse, or addiction, it's easier to avoid confusion.

Categories and Continua
Many use the term "addiction" without a formal definition, which can lead to misunderstandings. "Dependence" and "abuse" have specific meanings with acceptable discriminant validity, giving them the potential to improve communication. These terms should provide a convenient way for clinicians and researchers to communicate. Nevertheless, two people with the same diagnosis may not share a single symptom. A rigid focus on these diagnostic categories can also lead clinicians to miss a chance to prevent problems before they start. A client experiencing negative consequences might not qualify for any diagnosis but could still benefit from altering drug use. Thus, thinking about the impact of drugs on quality of life can prevent problems in a way that a premature focus on diagnoses might neglect.

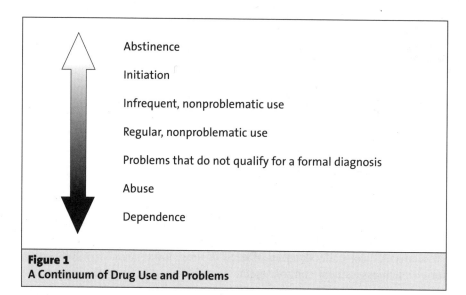

Figure 1
A Continuum of Drug Use and Problems

Unfortunately, lay conceptions of diagnostic categories confuse both clients and the public. For example, some people define any use of an illegal drug as abuse, but busy clinicians rarely have time to split hairs over who does or does not qualify for a label. Perhaps the best approach to defining misuse relies on cataloging problems that stem from the drug. This approach may provide the most specific information for treatment. Many view drug problems categorically – either substance use interferes with someone's life or it does not. Nevertheless, examining drug problems on a continuum has considerable utility and empirical support (Denson & Earleywine, 2006). One useful way to look at this range of troubles would place complete abstinence on one end of a continuum and serious problems, including abuse and dependence, on the other. Nonproblematic use might fall near the abstinence end of the continuum, while troubles that might not qualify for a diagnosis might lie closer to the diagnosable disorders. This continuous model might challenge those of us trained in the tradition of diagnosis or disease, but could also heighten awareness for the prevention of problems (see Figure 1). This continuous approach is also consistent with current calls for reformulation of the Diagnostic and Statistical Manual of Mental Disorders (DSM-IV;American Psychiatric Association, 1994).

Substance abuse problems can lie along a continuum

1.1.2 Common Drugs

Terms

Different psychoactive drugs can wax and wane in populartiy; it seems challenging to keep up with trends in use and the rituals and slang associated with new drugs. Nevertheless, a little effort can go a long way in clinical work. Clients appreciate therapists who know their world. Professionals with some background information about common drugs of abuse can gain credibility in their clients' eyes. Few therapists have time to become experts in every substance, but a general familiarity with commonly used drugs, the subjective effects that appear to motivate use, and common street names can prove helpful (see Table 1 for a focused list).

Subjective Effects

Subjective effects vary with dosage, expectations, experience and setting, so there are vast individual differences in response. An individualized approach is ideal, but general knowledge about substances can save clinicians time and effort. Drugs often produce certain effects as a result of straightforward physiological processes, so a few heuristics can apply across many drugs because we all share comparable nervous systems. Higher doses generally produce larger effects. For example, stimulants almost invariably increase heart rate, regardless of the user's beliefs or situation. This effect increases as the amount of the drug increases. Other effects arise, at least in part, because users believe these effects will occur. For example, those who believe that alcohol makes them more adept socially can feel more relaxed with others. Curiously, this social enhancement can arise even after drinking a placebo. In addition to expectations, a user's previous experience with a drug can alter the drug's impact. Those who have developed tolerance from prior use will experience a weaker effect from many drugs. In contrast, repeated exposure can make some individuals more sensitive to the negative consequences of drugs. For example, on the day after using MDMA, experienced users of the hallucinogen are more likely to report depressive symptoms than those who used the drug for the first time.

The intoxication experience also varies with setting. The same drug can have dramatically different effects in different circumstances. People who repeatedly

Subjective effects of drugs vary with dosage, set, setting, and experience

---

Table 1
Some Common Drugs, Reported Effects, and Street Names

Drug	Reported effects	Street names
Marijuana	Euphoria, laughter, hunger, sedation, aphrodisiac	Pot, grass, weed
Powder Cocaine	Stimulation, confidence, improved focus, aphrodisiac	Coke, dust, powder, flakes, coca, snow
Crack Cocaine	Extreme euphoria, stimulation, confidence	Crack, rock, sugar, bazooka, devil rocks
Heroin	Euphoria, sedation, analgesia	H, hard candy, dope, junk
Hallucinogens	Tangential thinking, perceptual aberrations, spiritual connection	Acid, X, candy, trips, 'shrooms
Inhalants	Laughter, analgesia, sedation	Rush, gas, huff, poppers,
Pain Relievers	Analgesia, euphoria, numbness	Oxy, Vics
Sedatives	Tranquility, relaxation	Reds, downers, downs
Stimulants	Increased arousal, improved focus	Uppers, ups, speed, crank, meth

use opiates in comparable settings can develop a conditioned tolerance to their effects, and the same dosage will fail to produce the euphoria or analgesia associated with earlier uses. This tolerance might not appear, however, when the drug is consumed in a different setting. Dramatic, sometimes lethal, sensitivity can return when individuals use the same drugs in the same amount but in a different environment. Setting can contribute to the subjective effects of a drug even independent of conditioning. Cannabis intoxication, for example, can feel relaxing in a group of friends but induce paranoia in a police station.

The subjective effects of drugs are difficult to describe but nearly all produce a reinforcing euphoria and relief from stress (Earleywine, 2005; see Table 1). Reactions to various drugs and the culture that often develops around them can be idiosyncratic. Clients often have their own slang, preferred effects, and other distinctions related to drugs. The street names of various drugs can change quickly in different eras and locations, too. Mental health professionals who let clients educate them about drugs often gain a great deal in little time. This information can prove useful for assessing drug use and for performing a functional analysis of the predictors and consequences of use. The most efficient way to learn about any drug is to ask clients about it directly.

1.1.3   Nonproblematic, Recreational Drug Use

Abstinence is easily defined as the complete absence of drug use. It makes an excellent anchor for the nonproblematic end of the drug use continuum. Fine distinctions moving from this end of the continuum to the problematic end, however, can generate heated debate. The idea that people can use drugs recreationally without negative consequences remains controversial despite the prevalence of controlled use of many psychoactive substances. The idea is worthy of our consideration, however, to prevent a premature or inappropriate focus on drug use when other problems might be more important for a specific client (Beck, Liese, & Najavits, 2005). For example, the modal consumer of alcohol drinks infrequently and rarely experiences so much as a hangover. The idea that people might use other drugs in a comparable way strikes some clinicians as odd. Many of us learned that certain drugs create inescapable biological changes that lead inexorably to problems. Data do not always support this idea (Julien, 2005); important individual differences exist. Unfortunately, we have no way of knowing if any specific person will make the transition from initiation of use of a drug to problematic use. In addition, the use of illicit drugs invariably carries more risk because of their potential to create trouble with the law.

Lifetime and Recent Use

Table 2 lists the percentage of Americans who use various drugs. These epidemiological data show that many people have used an illicit drug at least once in their lives, but relatively few have used one recently. Over 45% (more than 112 million) Americans have used an illicit drug, but only about 8% (less than 20 million) have used one in the last month. These data support two intriguing ideas: First, it is obvious that not all drug use leads inexorably to continued use. Clients who mention use of an illicit drug might actually experience no

Over 45% of Americans have tried an illicit drug

Table 2
Illicit Drug Use (Aged 12 or Older): Percentages

	Lifetime	Past Year	Past Month
All Illicit Drugs	46.1	14.4	8.1
Marijuana	40.1	10.4	6.0
Cocaine	13.8	2.3	1.0
Heroin	1.5	0.2	0.1
Hallucinogens	13.9	1.6	0.4
Inhalants	9.4	0.9	0.3
Pain Relievers	13.4	4.9	1.9
Sedatives	3.7	0.3	0.1
Stimulants	7.8	1.1	0.4

Source: Substance Abuse and Mental Health Services Administration (SAMHSA), 2006 National Survey on Drug Use and Health (Department of Health and Human Services, 2007)

negative consequences, and their therapy might not focus on drugs. Second, many clients with drug problems often emphasize that nearly everyone has tried illicit substances. Social psychology research on assumed similarity, the idea that others resemble ourselves, reveals that we all tend to guess that others behave as we do. Drug users are no exception. They are often surprised to learn that although many people have tried illicit drugs, few have used these drugs recently. Current users of illicit drugs are, in fact, in the minority.

1.1.4   Problematic Drug Use

Separating safer drug use from problematic use depends upon our definitions of problems. Distinguishing between problem-free and troubled drug use can prove difficult. Clients who consider themselves problem-free users frequently fail to attribute negative life events to drugs. Thus, they often describe their troubles to clinicians but fail to mention their consumption of substances. The stigma commonly associated with the use of illicit drugs can also make clients reluctant to mention them spontaneously. Mental health professionals who are familiar with the numerous substance-related diagnoses and different domains of drug problems invariably have a better chance of connecting drug use to negative life events. Although diagnostic systems differ, assessments of drug problems generally tap multiple domains. Most clients would like to build a life that includes a romantic partner, gratifying family relationships, close friends, satisfying work, financial stability, good health, delightful recreation, and a sense of personal development. Although the issue is often contentious, the popularity of 12-step approaches to problems has also led many clients and clinicians to reexamine the importance of a spiritual life and an appreciation for the divine. Drug use has the potential to interfere in all of these domains, making them appropriate targets for assessment. Most definitions of problems focus on at least some of these limitations to optimal functioning.

1.2   Definitions

The formal definitions for disordered drug use fall generally into categories of dependence and abuse (or harmful use). Clinicians apply the diagnoses reliably in many studies, but some of the nuances of symptoms are lost in the simple lists that often appear in publication or questionnaires. For example, raters agree quite well on diagnoses of abuse and dependence made from structured interviews (Ustün et al., 1997), but simplified questionnaires based on symptoms may lead to deviant estimates of the prevalence of these problems (Grant et al., 2007). Symptoms appear in the tables, with details below (American Psychiatric Association, 1994).

1.2.1   Dependence

The DSM-IV (American Psychiatric Association, 1994) defines drug dependence as any three or more of seven symptoms (see Table 3). These symptoms must create meaningful distress and occur within the same year. Each symptom reflects the idea that a person cannot function without the drug and makes maladaptive sacrifices to use it. Assessing these symptoms requires genuine clinical skill. Many clients associate drug use and related symptoms with stigma. A warm, nonjudgmental, empathic approach with questions that use straightforward, simple language will improve rapport and encourage candor (Beck et al., 2005). Frequent nods, smiles, and eye contact are essential, even when the clinician must take notes, as detailed in Section 3.

Focus on Consequences

The current dependence diagnosis focuses on consequences, not on the amount or frequency of consumption, and there are no hard and fast rules linking the quantity or regularity of use to a diagnosis. Dependence symptoms include tolerance (a decreased response to the same amount of a drug or a need for more to achieve the same effect), and withdrawal (a marked discomfort when the drug is not ingested), which were once considered the hallmarks of the

---

Clinical Pearl
Stimulant Withdrawal

A great many people who use stimulants problematically find withdrawal particularly aversive. Although fatigue would seem an obvious sign of stimulant withdrawal, some experience it as a jittery, nerve wracking, edgy feeling. These withdrawal symptoms can precede lapses. Oddly enough, some of the arousal that these people experience may stem from exaggerated caffeine and nicotine effects. Caffeine and nicotine are eliminated more slowly once other stimulants are no longer increasing a client's metabolism. This decreased metabolism may mean that doses of caffeine and nicotine that used to produce only minor effects now create whopping stimulation, which users often interpret as extreme withdrawal symptoms. An educational warning about this predicament may help users moderate their consumption of caffeine and nicotine and offer a reasonable explanation for some of the jitters they experience during withdrawal.

Table 3
Dependence Symptoms

1. Tolerance
2. Withdrawal
3. Use that exceeds intention
4. Failed attempts to quit or constant desire for the drug
5. Time lost
6. Reduced activities
7. Continued use despite problems

disorder. The DSM-IV distinguishes between dependence with and without a physiological component. If tolerance or withdrawal appear among the three required symptoms, a diagnosis of physiological dependence is appropriate. Nevertheless, even without tolerance or withdrawal, individuals may receive a diagnosis of substance dependence without a physiological component. That is, clients with three symptoms other than tolerance or withdrawal still qualify for the diagnosis. The additional symptoms include: use that exceeds initial intention, persistent desire for the drug or failed attempts to decrease consumption, a meaningful loss of time related to use, reduced activities because of consumption, and continued use despite problems. Over the years, diagnosticians can drift away from the formal definitions of these symptoms, so a review of their definitions can prove helpful.

1.2.2 Abuse

Many drug users experience negative consequences without qualifying for a dependence diagnosis. They still, however, might qualify for a diagnosis of abuse. Nevertheless, the discriminant validity of diagnoses of abuse and dependence is less than perfect (de Bruijn, Korzec, Koerselmann, & van Den Brink, 2004). Currently, the DSM-IV considers these two as separate diagnoses. Abuse specifically requires that the client does not qualify for dependence. (Most who qualify for dependence would also qualify for abuse, but the dependence diagnosis would take precedence under those circumstances.) Abuse requires significant, meaningful impairment or distress directly related to the use of the drug. Detectable dysfunction and strain are necessary to identify abuse. The general theme for the abuse diagnosis concerns a consequential interference with optimal performance because of negative consequences. The diagnosis requires only one of the four symptoms that appear in the current criteria in the DSM (American Psychiatric Association, 1994; see Table 4). These symptoms include one that overlaps with dependence: **continued use despite problems**. The other symptoms of dependence are: **interference with major obligations, intoxication in unsafe settings**, and **legal problems** (Ustün, et al., 1997).

Table 4
Abuse Symptoms

1. Continued use despite problems
2. Interference with major obligations
3. Intoxication in an unsafe setting
4. Repeated legal problems

1.2.3   Codes from the Diagnostic and Statistical Manual

DSM Codes for drug-related disorders vary with drug of choice

The DSM provides an extensive list of categories based on the drug of choice as well as whether a particular client is experiencing intoxication, dependence, or abuse. The decision to include intoxication for some drugs but not others has generated some controversy. The notion that intoxication alone might qualify as a disorder has also created considerable debate. Given the prevalence of the use of multiple substances, a category of polysubstance dependence also appears (see Table 5).

Table 5
Substance-Related Codes from the DSM

303.00 Alcohol Intoxication

303.90 Alcohol Dependence

304.00 Opioid Dependence

304.10 Sedative, Hypnotic, or Anxiolytic Dependence

304.20 Cocaine Dependence

304.30 Cannabis Dependence

304.40 Amphetamine Dependence

304.50 Hallucinogen Dependence

304.60 Inhalant Dependence

304.60 Phencyclidine Dependence

304.80 Polysubstance Dependence

304.90 Other (or Unknown) Substance Dependence

305.00 Alcohol Abuse

305.10 Nicotine Dependence

305.20 Cannabis Abuse

305.30 Hallucinogen Abuse

305.40 Sedative, Hypnotic, or Anxiolytic Abuse

305.50 Opioid Abuse

Table 5 (continued)

305.60 Cocaine Abuse

305.70 Amphetamine Abuse

305.90 Caffeine Intoxication

305.90 Inhalant Abuse

305.90 Other (or Unknown) Substance Abuse

305.9 Phencyclidine Abuse

1.2.4   Drug Problems

Many drug-related troubles do not serve as formal symptoms of any diagnosis, but an astute clinician and a willing client can view these as opportunities to prevent further problems. Candid discussions often reveal volatile or estranged relationships with family and friends that can arise from conflict about drug use, financial problems, or other behaviors related to substance abuse. These would all suggest less than optimal functioning even if these individuals do not quite qualify for any of the diagnostic categories mentioned above. Popular assessment devices ask about problems with physical and mental health, social skills, family functioning, school and work, peer relationships, and leisure.

1.3   Epidemiology

1.3.1   World Statistics

Estimating how many people use illicit drugs can prove daunting because of the potential for self-report bias. Many large epidemiological studies rely on phone interviews that participants might not perceive as particularly anonymous. Estimates of use might be underestimates given the understandable tendency to avoid admitting to an illegal behavior. Worldwide estimates of the number of people who used an illicit drug in the past year remain around 200 million. The number who have used in the past month is smaller, around 110 million.

Marijuana remains the most prevalent illicit drug across nations; the stimulants and opiates are used markedly less often (Degenhardt et al., 2008). Reported rates of illicit drug use can vary dramatically across different countries, with Asia reporting dramatically lower rates (Devaney, Reid, & Baldwin, 2007). These comparisons across countries require cautious interpretation, however, as variations in penalties and associated stigma may contribute to different rates of underreporting. Demand for treatment focuses on the opiates in Asia, cannabis in Africa, and cocaine in South America, suggesting that availability is the best predictor of drug of choice.

As Table 2 demonstrates, the prevalence of illicit drug use has received considerable attention in the US. Over 45% of people have used illicit drugs at some time in their lives, with marijuana the most common and heroin the least. Rates of use vary dramatically across the different drugs, perhaps as a function of perceived risk of negative consequences. More people try drugs that are perceived to be less harmful. Polydrug use is common. Use of one illicit drug tends to predict use of another (Tetrault et al., 2008), so the total percentage of drug users is smaller than the sum of the users for each drug.

1.3.2   Demographic Correlates

A slightly different data set reveals that rates of use vary with gender, age, and ethnicity (see Table 6). Currently, a higher percentage of men than women have tried illicit drugs. Young adults aged 18–25 are more likely to have used a drug in their lifetime than people of other age groups. In addition, a higher percentage of Native Americans have used a drug than members of other ethnic groups. Theories for these links to gender, age, and ethnicity focus on everything from the physiological to the societal.

Table 6
Rates of Illicit Drug Initiation By Demographics (in percentages)

Demographic Characteristic	Lifetime
Total	45.4
Age	
12–17	27.6
18–25	59.0
26 or older	45.5
Gender	
Male	50.3
Female	40.9
Hispanic origin and race	
Not Hispanic or Latino	47.1
White	49.0
Black or African American	42.9
American Indian or Alaska Native	58.8
Native Hawaiian or Other Pacific Islander	40.9
Asian	23.7
Two or More Races	55.4
Hispanic or Latino	35.0

From National Survey on Drug Use and Health (DHHS; 2007)

1.3.3   Recent Use

The majority of lifetime use is experimental (Department of Health and Human Services, 2007). Despite the large percentage of people who have tried an illicit drug at some time, the number who have used in the past month is remarkably small (see Table 7). This fact often comes as a surprise to current users, who frequently overestimate the prevalence of current drug use. Fewer than 1 in 10 U.S. citizens reported using an illicit drug other than marijuana in the past month, and 1 in 100 or fewer reported using hallucinogens, inhalants, methamphetamine, crack, or heroin.

Table 7
Drug Use by U.S. Citizens Age 12 and Over (Percentages)

Drug	Lifetime	Past Month
Marijuana	39.8	14.8
Illicit drugs other than marijuana	29.6	9.6
Nonmedical use of prescription drugs	20.3	7.0
Cocaine (including crack)	14.3	2.4
Hallucinogens	14.3	1.0
Inhalants	9.3	0.8
Methamphetamine	5.8	0.7
Crack	3.5	0.7
Heroin	1.5	0.3

From DHHS (2007)

1.3.4   Abuse and Dependence

Rates for abuse and dependence are markedly smaller than these rates for lifetime or recent use (Compton, Thomas, Stinson, & Grant, 2007). Face-to-face interviews with over 40,000 U.S. residents revealed that 12-month drug abuse prevalence was 1.4% and lifetime abuse was 7.7%. Rates of dependence were even lower at 0.6% for past year and 2.6% for lifetime. Abuse and dependence are markedly less common than use. Other Axis I disorders, particularly the anxiety and mood disorders, are also much more common than abuse and dependence. Lifetime rates for anxiety are around 29%, with 18% affected in a given year. For mood disorders, lifetime rates are approximately 21% with approximately 10% affected in a given year. Rates of abuse and dependence varied with demographics in ways comparable to use. Men, Native Americans, and those aged 18–44 received diagnoses more often. In addition, those who lived in the Western US, those with fewer financial resources, and those who were unmarried were also more likely to receive a diagnosis. Seeking treatment or help of any kind was remarkably rare, with only 8.1% of those with an

Lifetime rates for abuse and dependence are 7.7% and 2.6% respectively

abuse diagnosis and 37.9% of those with a dependence diagnosis reporting any sort of assistance for drug-related problems. The majority of those with drug abuse or dependence do not seek outside help (Compton et al., 2007).

1.4   Course and Prognosis

The course and prognosis for those with drug abuse, dependence, and problems varies dramatically from person to person, across time, and for different drugs. A candid summary reveals the inherent difficulties associated with treating these troubles but leaves room for optimism about each individual client. About two-thirds of those who meet diagnostic criteria for substance abuse disorder now will not meet those criteria three years later, even though few of them receive formal treatment (Heyman, 1996).

1.4.1   Chronicity

Relapse is common among problem users who appear for treatment (Anglin, Connor, Annon, & Longshore 2007). Many who use drugs problematically continue to do so for years. But our perceptions of the frequency of these problems may reflect biases. We think of drug abuse as a chronic, relapsing disorder because only people with the chronic, relapsing form of drug abuse disorder appear for treatment. Others identify problems early in the course of use and refrain from further consumption of drugs. Many others fall somewhere in between. Most drug use, both licit and illicit, begins in adolescence. Earlier onset of use remains one of the best predictors of problems. Those who use drugs when they are younger are more likely to receive abuse and dependence diagnoses. The reason for this association between youth and problems remains unclear. Researchers have hypothesized mechanisms ranging from drug-induced interruption of brain development, age-related biases in diagnoses, and interference in the development of coping skills. Thus, delaying the onset of drug use may be an ideal tactic for the prevention of problems. Similarly, early intervention with teens who have initiated drug use has enormous potential for improving public health.

1.5   Differential Diagnosis

Diagnosing almost any disorder requires an assessment of drug use both licit and illicit. Aspects of intoxication, withdrawal, and chronic use overlap so much with symptoms of psychopathology that the chance of mistaking drug-related problems for common disorders is simply too high. The problem is particularly salient for disorders related to deviant arousal and disordered thought. Thus, it is essential to ensure that intoxication and withdrawal have subsided before any attempts to make diagnoses of other disorders (Davis, Uezato, Newell, & Frazier, 2008).

1.5.1   Deviant Arousal

Although problems related to drug use can often look like other psychiatric disorders, a thorough, candid assessment can minimize any problems related to differential diagnosis. Understanding how the acute and chronic effects of individual drugs can mimic symptoms of other disorders can prove helpful. A first dimension of drug effects concerns arousal. Acute use of stimulants increase arousal; chronic use and withdrawal can decrease arousal. Sedatives and opiates can also decrease arousal. With these effects in mind, it is easy to see how certain drugs can mimic anxiety and mood disorders. The acute, heavy use of stimulants can create panic and general anxiety. A stimulant binge can mimic mania and eventually create psychotic symptoms including paranoia and delusions. Alternating periods of intoxication and withdrawal can resemble cyclothymia, particularly when clients are willing to discuss their moods but not their drug use.

Differential diagnosis can prove particularly difficult when the drugs of abuse are not illicit ones. Clients with obvious symptoms of panic or anxiety often fail to realize that consuming 14 cups of coffee per day might exacerbate their symptoms. A listless, depressed young man who would ordinarily be full of energy might fail to mention that he has recently doubled his allergy medication and over-the-counter antihistamines. A chronic pain patient might report inexplicable bouts of moody weeping and euphoric bliss but not connect these symptoms to the changing of a fentanyl patch. Thorough assessments of the frequency and timing of symptoms as well as the use of any drug, licit or illicit, can help circumvent these problems.

1.5.2   Thought Disorder

Another relevant effect of drugs concerns disordered thought of various kinds. The hallucinogens, as their name implies, can produce perceptual aberrations similar to those seen in psychotic disorders. They also create some of the deviant thought processes common to psychosis. Withdrawal from alcohol and other sedatives can lead to hallucinations comparable to those seen in schizophrenia. Despite these difficulties, drug abuse, dependence, and problems are often easy to identify despite these shared symptoms with other disorders simply because drug disorders require the ingestion of substances (Beck et al., 2005). The problems with differential diagnosis that stem from inaccurate or incomplete information on drug use drive home the importance of encouraging client candor through detailed and enthusiastic explanations of confidentiality. Several minutes spent explaining confidentiality, particularly in our current era of complex and confusing HIPAA forms, can save hours later when clients are more forthcoming about their drug use. Despite the relative ease of differential diagnosis, issues related to comorbidity are markedly more complicated.

1.6   Comorbidities

Studies of the general population as well as treatment samples reveal considerable overlap between drug problems and other disorders, especially those related to impulse control, mood, anxiety, and personality. Trained raters using a structured assessment device known as the Psychiatric Research Interview for Substance and Mental Disorders for DSM-IV (PRISM-IV) have reliably diagnosed disorders that frequently occur in conjunction with drug problems (Hasin et al., 2006). Co-occurring disorders often predict poor prognosis (e.g., Shane, Jasiukaitis, & Green, 2003). The high rates of comorbidity can lead clinicians to wonder whether to treat drug problems prior to other disorders or vice versa. Because many aspects of therapy for a variety of problems share common features, this distinction can seem artificial. For example, challenging maladaptive cognitions related to depression is comparable to challenging cognitions related to drug use. Many professionals prefer to get clients to decrease or stop their substance use in an effort to see what symptoms remain once drugs are no longer contributing to a patient's behavior. In fact, decreasing the frequency of intoxication can have a dramatic impact on the symptoms of other disorders. Decreasing the negative consequences of drug use will improve functioning in multiple domains and help the symptoms of other problems as well. In contrast, some problems, especially bipolar disorder and the psychoses, may require treatment prior to or simultaneously with the substance abuse treatment.

1.6.1   Impulse control disorders

Drug problems often co-occur with problems of impulse control

Problem gambling, eating disorders, attention deficit disorder, childhood conduct disorder, as well as antisocial and borderline personality all covary with drug problems (Compton et al., 2007). Generally, each of these disorders involves problems inhibiting a dominant response to avoid negative consequences. Failing to resist a first impulse leads to trouble. In this sense, these disorders are very similar to giving in to the urge to use drugs frequently or excessively.

1.6.2   Problem Gambling

At least a third and often more than half of problem gamblers report drug problems, and the interaction of these two challenging behaviors can create a disturbing downward spiral (Petry & Pietrzak, 2004). Drowning sorrows related to losses can lead to intoxication, which impairs judgment, potentially contributing to more and riskier betting, increased financial problems, and an increased risk for more drug use. Curiously, winning at gambling can also lead to celebratory use of drugs that can also increase further gambling, creating a greater risk for more losses and more substance use. The euphoria associated with intoxication can also create inaccurate assessments of abilities or probabilities, leading to risky speculation of many sorts. Treatments for these drug and gambling problems can go hand in hand, as decreased frequency of intoxication can help keep betting to a minimum, which can in turn decrease the temptation to use drugs.

1.6.3   Eating Disorders

In addition to problem gambling, eating disorders and drug use co-occur often, particularly among women (see Anderson, Simmons, Martens, Ferrrier, & Sheehy, 2006). Clients with eating disorders often abuse stimulant drugs, which have known anorectic effects. Clients often claim to turn to these drugs in an effort to keep their appetites suppressed. People report using caffeine and nicotine as well as illicit stimulants for this same purpose, often despite overwhelming evidence that the long-term impact on the amount of food consumed is negligible. Long drug-induced fasts often end with binges that lead to negative affect and the temptation to use more drugs or eat more. Excessive alcohol use is common among clients with eating disorders as well. Both intoxication and binge eating may serve as maladaptive ways to cope with negative emotions (Luce, Engler, & Crowther, 2007). Learning new skills for tolerating distress can improve drug problems and troubled eating, potentially diminishing concerns about which disorder to treat first. Nevertheless, decreasing intoxication can likely decrease binges, laxative abuse, and fasting (Gadalla & Piran, 2007). These behaviors might serve as manifestations of an inability to inhibit dominant responses, much like the issues inherent in attention-deficits and other inhibitory problems.

1.6.4   Attention Deficit Disorders

Although drug-related links with attention deficit disorder vary for hyperactive, inattentive, and compulsive symptoms, children with attention deficit disorder are at increased risk for initiating the use of substances. They also may be more likely to develop symptoms of dependence or abuse, depending upon the presence of conduct disorder (Looby, 2008). People may turn to drugs as an attempt to self-medicate problems with attention or because of a general tendency to take risks and experiment with novelty. Pharmacological treatments for childhood ADHD do not appear to increase risk for subsequent drug problems, and some of these medications show promise in helping subsets of adults decrease substance abuse (Castells et al., 2007). Separating the ADHD from the impact of drug use requires careful assessment. The presence of symptoms in the absence of intoxication or withdrawal can support an ADHD diagnosis. Report of symptoms that appeared prior to drug use can also confirm ADHD. Although ADHD does predict later drug use, the magnitude of the effect may not be as large as researchers once thought. Early work on the impact of ADHD on drug use and problems was also confounded by comorbid conduct disorder.

1.6.5   Conduct Disorder

The impact of conduct disorder on substance initiation and problems is even larger than the effect for ADHD (Looby, 2008). Both conduct disorder and illicit drug use may reflect a broad disrespect for legal and societal sanctions (Elkins, McGue, & Iacono, 2007). Although current treatments for conduct disorder are often ineffective, decreasing drug use can help decrease problem behaviors associated with the disorder. Conduct disorder appears to stem from problems in the functioning of the prefrontal area of the brain (Ishikawa & Raine, 2003). Deficits in this area may also lead to substance abuse, which can further impair the same areas that would normally help inhibit the desire to use drugs (Lyvers, 2000). Thus, drug use can exacerbate the small deficits that led to drug use in the first place, leading to further consumption, more deficits, and still more drug use. Given the link between conduct disorder and antisocial personality disorder, it's not surprising that the latter leads to an increased likelihood of drug problems as well as an increase in their severity (see Westermeyer & Thuras, 2005).

1.6.6   Personality Disorders

Many personality disorders co-occur with substance abuse problems. The majority of the research on this topic focuses on the Cluster B diagnoses, particularly antisocial and borderline personality disorder. Antisocial personality disorder and the use of illicit substances often go hand in hand (Simmons & Havens, 2007). Many clinicians view the treatment of antisocial personality disorder with considerable pessimism. People with this diagnosis and substance use disorders do show more legal and family problems than clients in drug treatment who do not have the personality disorder (Westermeyer & Thuras, 2005). Nevertheless, substance abusing clients with antisocial personality disorder are no different from other substance abusers on many other measures of troubles. Decreasing the frequency and intensity of intoxication has the potential to limit aggression, crime, and other antisocial acts. Some studies suggest that these behaviors remit with age, so minimizing them in an effort to keep young people out of the legal system can pay off tremendously in the long run (Black, 2007).

Borderline personality disorder and substance abuse are highly comorbid. The combination does not bode well for treatment, primarily because people with both disorders are more likely than not to drop out (Bornovalova & Daughters, 2007). Borderline personality disorder accompanies difficulty in regulating emotion. Intoxication undoubtedly can create positive mood temporarily, but most drugs have a biphasic effect in which initial delight turns to irritation and sorrow later. This sort of subacute withdrawal can prove particularly intolerable to those who have trouble regulating their moods in other ways. Moods can become more predictable when drug use is kept to a minimum. Even caffeine and nicotine can create fairly dramatic alterations in affect (Julien, 2005). Decreasing drug use as part of a larger set of behaviors aimed at improved mood regulation will help people with borderline personality disorder feel better and potentially diminish many other problematic behaviors, including self-harm (Linehan, 1993).

1.6.7   Mood Disorders

Because drugs have such a dramatic impact on mood, people with mood disorders are likely to use substances. People with drug problems are more likely to report mood disorders, and people with mood disorders are more likely to report drug problems. Up to 60% of people diagnosed with a mood disturbance also report a substance abuse problem (Flynn & Brown, 2008; Kessler & Wang, 2008).The majority of the work on this topic focuses on depression and bipolar disorder. Nevertheless, links between substance use and cyclothymia or dysthymia also exist. Although diagnosing mood disorders in people who currently use substances can prove difficult, extended abstinence can help identify whether symptoms arise from a mood disorder. Clients who report a depressive episode prior to drug use often see little improvement in mood despite supervised abstinence, but clients without such a history often see dramatic changes in mood in only a couple of weeks. A careful look at retrospective reports of symptom onset can also help separate mood disorders from persistent intoxication or withdrawal. These findings support the idea of limiting drug use prior to treating depressive symptoms (Nunes & Levin, 2006). Manic episodes induced by stimulant abuse can decrease dramatically once drug use disappears, but if the mania actually arose because of bipolar disorder, pharmacological treatments for bipolar can actually help clients maintain abstinence.

Drug problems often accompany mood and anxiety disorders

1.6.8   Anxiety Disorders

Drug abuse and dependence is quite common among people with anxiety disorders. Generalized anxiety disorder, posttraumatic stress disorder, social anxiety, phobia, agoraphobia, panic, and even separation anxiety co-occur with substance abuse and dependence (Grant et al., 2007). The link between anxiety and drug use can depend on expectations about a drug's anxiolytic effects. Those who believe a drug will decrease their anxiety are often the ones who are most likely to use drugs as their anxiety increases. Despite successful behavioral treatments for anxiety, a great many people with these disorders choose pharmacotherapy, potentially increasing some of the expectation that drugs will help. The interplay between anxiety and withdrawal symptoms can make treatment particularly tricky. For example, cigarette smokers with panic disorder report more motivation to smoke to relieve negative emotions, and may confuse nicotine withdrawal for panic symptoms, potentially increasing rates of relapse. Although the evidence is mixed, treatments for anxiety disorders during substance abuse treatment have significant potential (Zvolensky et al., 2005). Helping clients separate withdrawal symptoms from anxiety or panic is time well spent.

1.6.9   Suicide

Drug-related problems increase the chances of suicidal ideation, suicide attempts, and completed suicide. These increases are large and meaningful. For example, problem heroin users are more than 10 times as likely to attempt suicide as controls (Harris & Barraclough, 1997). Despite low rates of suicide attempts in the general population, various studies reveal one fifth to one half of drug dependent individuals have suicidal ideation. Up to one third of drug abusers in treatment have attempted suicide (Ries, Yuodelis-Flores, Comtois, Roy-Byrne, & Russo, 2008). Those at greatest risk have a previous attempt as well as other self-injurious behavior. Despite clinical impressions to the contrary, interventions can prove effective at preventing suicide. Even brief outpatient treatments can decrease self-injury and need not require hospital stays or great expense (Comtois & Linehan, 2006).

1.7   Diagnostic Procedures and Documentation

The list of potential assessment instruments is long and varied (see Table 8). Each focuses on different aspects of predictors of use, consumption, and consequences. Details about administering comparable assessments appear in Section 3 (Diagnosis and Treatment Indications). Generally, the assessments are face-to-face interviews or paper-and-pencil questionnaires. The interviews invariably require all the standard recommendations for building rapport, encouraging candid responses, and decreasing defensiveness. The questionnaires can sometimes lead to increased accuracy, particularly for difficult topics that cause clients shame or embarrassment. They can also prove helpful when staff time is limited and clients have good reading skills. As with a clinical interview, it is important to stress the confidentiality of these questionnaires to encourage honest and accurate responses.

Table 8
Measures of Drug Use, Associated Problems, and Treatment-Relevant Factors

Interviews
- Diagnostic and Statistical Manual (DSM) Interview Schedule – assesses symptoms for abuse and dependence diagnoses for different drugs (First, Spitzer, Gibbon, & Williams, 1996)
- Timeline Follow-back (TLFB) – assesses quantity and frequency of use of substances (Sobell & Sobell, 2005)
- Maudsley Addiction Profile – assesses negative consequences of drugs across multiple domains (Marsden et al., 1998)

Questionnaires
- Severity of Dependence Questionnaire – a brief assessment of withdrawal, tolerance, and associated concerns about dependence (Stockwell, Murphy, & Hodgson, 1983)

Drug-specific problem inventories
- Cannabis Problems Questionnaire (Copeland, Gilmour, Gates, & Swift, 2005)
- Marijuana Screening Inventory (Alexander & Leung, 2006)
- Cocaine Effects Questionnaire (Rohsenow, Sirota, Martin, & Monti, 2004)
- Drug Use Screening Inventory (Kirisci, Tarter, Mezzich, & Reynolds, 2008)

2

The Biopsychosocial Model of Drug Problems

Etiological work on substance-related problems can inform treatment in helpful ways. It has generated prevention and intervention efforts that address
issues as large as international policy and as small as pharmacotherapies that
focus on individual neurotransmitter systems.

Multiple factors contribute to drug use, problems, and treatment outcome

Theories of drug problems have a long history, beginning with conceptual-
izations that relied on evil spirits, moral weakness, and complex intrapsychic
conditions that proved impossible to measure. Many early theories emphasized
a particular domain of contributors to the exclusion of others, making them
inadequate in their account of problems. A myopic, restricted focus on any
one dimension, whether spiritual, medical, psychological, or societal, led to
missing important aspects of problems. Treatments based on these theories
invariably neglected aspects of the person and failed to improve some domain
of associated problems. An alternative approach designed to encompass more
of the potential contributors to drug problems developed in an effort to account
for the multifaceted nature of human experience – the biopsychosocial model
(Mosey, 1974).

The predominant model of drug problems attempts to incorporate findings from disparate literatures ranging from the cellular to the societal. These
efforts to explain substance abuse and dependence have interesting implications for prevention and treatment, and advantages over previous work that
focused exclusively on single domains. The heterogeneity of drug-related
disorders makes constructing an all-encompassing model quite challenging.
The different interacting biological, psychological, and social contributors can
be easier to understand in light of different stages of drug use (see Figure 2).
Different facets of each contributor can have a different effect on each of these
stages and the transition from one stage to the next.

One way to view stages of drug use begins with no use and extends to
problematic use as well as treatment outcome. The vast majority of people
begin life with little exposure to drugs. A subset of those initiate drug use
depending upon various factors. A group of those people continues subsequent
use of drugs. A subset of this group then develops problems. A handful of these
people receive treatment, with a variety of outcomes. The transitions from no
use to problematic use to treatment outcome each rest on different kinds and
degrees of biological, psychological, and social variables.

2.1   Interacting Components

As the name suggests, the biopsychosocial model rests on potentially heritable physiological components. Substance use disorders clearly run in families; twin studies support a strong contribution of genetics (Agrawal & Lynskey, 2008; Hicks et al., 2007). The heritable component might include genes that contribute to out-of-the-ordinary neurotransmitter function, drug metabolism, or sensitivity to stimuli. These qualities alone need not be deficits; in fact, they may provide distinct advantages in certain settings. Inheriting a novel desire for adventure or a tendency to avoid harm might prove adaptive in some environments but lead to drug problems in others (Julien, 2005). Because substance abuse and dependence are among a handful of disorders in the DSM that require something outside of the individual (in this case, drugs) for the diagnosis, the psychological, social, and societal components can prove particularly important. No single gene or biological factor absolutely predicts the future occurrence of drug problems (Buckland, 2008). In addition, some situations might lead to drug problems regardless of an individual's biological makeup. Repeated exposure to some drugs, particularly the opiates, almost invariably leads to small increases in tolerance and withdrawal regardless of physiological variation among people. Abuse and dependence only arise as a result of a combination of these physiological, psychological, and social factors.

2.2   Initiation

Separating who will and who will not try a drug depends upon a complex set of biological, societal, and psychological phenomena. The majority of the work on the initiation of drug use looks at school-aged youth. Generally, the availability of the drug, personality, family functioning, socioeconomic stressors, trauma, parental attitudes and use, peer attitudes and use, religiosity, alternative reinforcing activities, and psychopathology contribute. The biological component of initiation may rest on the heritable tendency to seek thrills or fail to control impulses as well as any genetic propensity toward disorders that frequently covary with drug problems. Social policies that create uncontrollable underground markets and various forms of social stressors may put some citizens at particular risk. Modeling from family members, peers, and media alter expectancies and attitudes about drugs. Potential buffers against initiation include religious observance, academic successes, and participation in organized sports. These biological, societal, and psychological factors are rarely assigned to people at random, so spurious links between some of these variables and drug problems may exist. In addition, the specificity of these factors to drug problems in particular is probably low. These conditions not only predict the initiation of drug use but a host of other problem behaviors, including aggression, unsafe sex, teen pregnancy, and school dropout (Clayton, Segress, & Caudill, 2008).

2.3   Regular Use

Multiple biological, psychological, social, and societal factors interact to impact the transition from initiation to regular use. A promising candidate for what seems to be inherited is the biological predisposition for a response to the drugs themselves. Several lines of research suggest that individuals vary dramatically in their acute responses to drugs. Even morphine and oxycodone, opiate drugs with legendary reputations for producing euphoria, actually delight some users while nauseating others (Zacny & Lictor, 2008). Hangover and acute withdrawal from drugs also appears to vary with biological factors. These withdrawal symptoms may motivate subsequent use to alleviate distress in some individuals, but turn others away from the drug completely. These physiological reactions that appear after the first initiation of drug use contribute to repetition of use. A number of opiate users describe their first use in idealized terms. Nevertheless, a minimal or even adverse initial reaction alone might not buffer an individual against becoming a regular user. Social factors may override these biological reactions in interesting ways. A number of Asian drinkers report aversive flushing in response to their first exposure to alcohol, but social pressures led to continued consumption (Nakawatase, Yamamoto, & Sasao, 1993). Most first-time users of cannabis claim little or no effect but regular users claim they persisted in the absence of a positive experience because other users were so effusive about the plant's effects. Stories of initial uses of cigarettes usually include queasiness and vomiting. Those who continued to use despite these experience often claim that they did so because friends emphasized that the experience improved. Research suggests that biological factors may contribute not only to the acute effects of drugs but also the subsequent craving for these drugs (Adinoff, 2004). These factors may also contribute to the transition to regular use.

2.4   Problem Use

The subsequent change from regular use to problem use also depends on various biological, psychological, and social factors. A physiological disposition might separate those who are prone to drug-induced health problems of many types. The tendency to develop abuse and dependence symptoms also appears heritable. In addition, psychological aspects of personality, stress reactivity, and expectancies play an important role in the development of troubles. For example, regular use tends to escalate to dependence more rapidly in women than in men (Becker & Hu, 2008), potentially for a combination of physiological, psychological, and social reasons. In addition, those who are more disinhibited or sensation seeking may not only initiate drug use more often but also continue to use until problems develop. Those who experience dramatic decreases in tension in response to drugs, or those who simply believe that they do, seem to be at greater risk for problem use. People who have more education, more training in alternative leisure activities, and better financial resources appear to have less risk of developing drug problems, even among frequent users.

2.5   Treatment Outcomes

All of these factors contribute to recovery from problems. For a multitude of reasons, offspring of substance abusers have different treatment outcomes. People with quality social support, improved financial conditions, better physical and mental health, and intact cognitive abilities may be much more likely to improve with treatment than others (Trafton, Tracy, Olivia, & Humphreys, 2007). The interaction of multiple factors has contributed to the development of certain treatment approaches, particularly pharmacological interventions that work in tandem with psychological treatments, therapeutic communities, and even altered societal policies. Factors as diverse as physiological blockers of drug effects to legal sanctions that lead to therapy instead of incarceration rely on these multimodal approaches to treatment outcome.

A key feature of the biopsychosocial model concerns the interactions among these contributors. A biological propensity to experience a drug as reinforcing must interact with the opportunity to initiate use, which likely arises from psychological factors like stress or initial expectations about a drug's effect as well as social factors like the drug's availability. A biological predisposition to enjoy thrills may contribute to the choice of social settings where drugs are available. Continued use can then alter biological functioning. Heavy use of certain drugs can impair cognitive functioning, decreasing the ability to resist subsequent use. Consistent use and associated problems may alter the social environment, leading users to spend more time with other users, altering their perceptions about how common drug consumption actually is. Continued use also may alter mood, perceptions of the self, and other psychological factors that might further increase a reliance on drugs. The subsequent persistence of use might then create more biological changes, altering psychological and social factors further, thereby repeating the cycle.

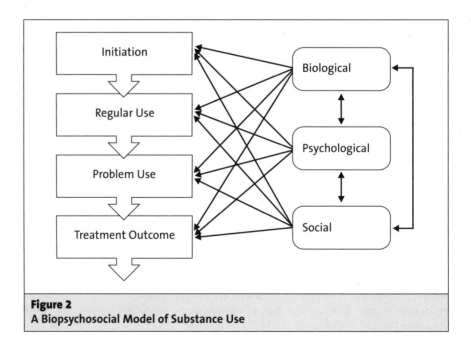

Figure 2
A Biopsychosocial Model of Substance Use

3

Diagnosis, Assessment and Treatment Indications

The symptoms for diagnosing abuse and dependence appeared in Section 1. The current section focuses on assessments of detailed drug use, problems, and motivation to change, each of which will prove helpful for ongoing treatment.

3.1   General Guidelines

3.1.1   Assessment IS treatment

For ease of discussion, assessment often means gathering information, whereas therapy refers to the potentially curative interactions between client and clinician. This assessment and therapy can then combine to form treatment (Beck et al., 2005). Researchers and clinicians sometimes assume that therapy is neatly sandwiched between periods of assessment, when in reality the distinction between them is usually arbitrary. Some treatment manuals further promote this assumption by implying that the "real therapy" only begins after clients complete extensive assessment batteries to determine the extent of their problems. Weeks or months later, another extensive set of assessments purportedly reveals if therapy has succeeded. Clients and therapists alike can often forget that assessment remains an essential part of treatment. In fact, assessment and therapy go hand in hand. This interactive nature of assessment and therapy means that some assessment techniques will appear during moments that many would consider therapy. This situation suggests that the best assessments build rapport, show empathy, and help the development of a therapeutic relationship. In addition, therapy might be best when it turns to assessments of well-operationalized signs, symptoms, problems, and goals.

A formal assessment provides valuable information on multiple topics, including drugs used, their quantities, the frequency of their use, and some of the situations that predict consumption. These assessments have the potential to help clients recognize the magnitude of their use and associated problems. Structured assessments can maintain the empathy, warmth, and genuineness of therapy. In fact, this approach can generate considerable trust. Given established biases in self-reports of controversial behaviors (LaBrie & Earleywine, 2003), increasing trust is likely to help clinicians get more accurate information. These formal, structured tasks can prove more important than the heart-to-heart chats that stereotypes of therapy can suggest. Many clients who think that they use drugs only occasionally can find that a candid assessment turns into an eye-opening experience.

The validity of self-reports of drug use can be extremely good. Self-reports covary reasonably with biochemical tests like hair and urine analysis (see Ledgerwood, Goldberger, Risk, Lewis, & Price, 2008). They also can align well with the reports of collaterals (Stasiewicz et al., 2008). These reports tend to improve when the negative consequences for reporting drug use are minimal or when anonymity is high (Fendrich, Mackesy-Amiti, Johnsons, Hubbell, & Wislar, 2005; LaBrie & Earleywine, 2003). The validity can vary, however, with a host of contributors. Age, gender, ethnicity, drug of choice, and the location of the test can alter the validity of the self-reports. For example, older Caucasian women may prove more willing to report accurately than other participants (see Sloan, Bodapati, & Tucker, 2004). Respondents with more severe drug problems may under-report the most. Those with severe mental illnesses like psychotic or bipolar disorders can be particularly inaccurate in their responses (Stasiewicz et al., 2008). All of this research emphasizes that a nonjudgmental approach is best for these assessments.

Maintaining focus during formal assessment sessions, when the primary goal is to gather information, can be an art. Sometimes clients long to tell detailed stories of every event that surrounded a particular episode of use. These tales can serve as great sources of data for identifying cues for relapse that will be useful later in treatment. Nevertheless, they can also consume valuable time and prevent accurate and complete assessments. For this portion of treatment, a consistent focus on use and consequences will pay off in the end. A simple explanation to clients that the current session will be devoted to detailing use can work wonders for keeping the assessment on track. Gentle reminders that treatment will return to other topics once the assessment is complete can also prove very helpful. Even when initial sessions are devoted to assessment almost exclusively, subsequent sessions will essentially begin with brief assessments as well, whether it be a formal questionnaire or a casual "How's it going?"

Explanations of a few assessment devices can provide general principles that apply to most others and will likely prove useful throughout therapy. The remaining portions of this section will focus on an interview (The Timeline Follow-Back; TLFB), a questionnaire (The Inventory of Drug Use Consequences; InDUC), the single item Motivation for Change Ruler, and continue with assessments of treatment history and social support.

3.2 A Note on Taking Notes

Clinicians and researchers are so accustomed to taking notes that the peculiarity of the process can escape them. Few personal interactions include anyone taking notes. Talking one-on-one about personal problems can be odd enough. When another person opens a notebook in the middle of the process, it can feel exceptionally odd for the client. It's easy for clients to think mistakenly that somehow the notes are more important than they are. Even demonstration films of exemplary therapists can reveal them holding notes in front of their faces in a distracted, preoccupied way. Maintaining regular eye contact, empathic body posture, and signs of interest is essential in this process. Simple requests and explanations go a long way to normalize the assessment process. "Mind if I take some notes?" is a splendid introduction to the process. Comments like: "These'll help me complete your insurance forms," or "We'll have a list of ideas you can take home when you're done," can make the notes seem less bizarre.

3.3   The Timeline Follow-Back (TLFB)

One intuitively appealing and informative assessment of drug use is the Timeline Follow-Back, a retrospective examination that has proven reliable and valid over lengthy periods in literally dozens of studies (Sobell & Sobell, 2000). Research has focused on periods as brief as two weeks or as long as a year. Clients review a calendar and use memory aids to create a detailed record of their drug use (see Figure 3). Information on the specific date, drugs used, and amounts consumed lays a superb foundation for subsequent work identifying tough times for risk for relapse. A date book can prove invaluable for this assessment, though many clients with serious drug problems laugh heartily when asked about keeping an appointment calendar. Any memory of holidays, birthdays, special events, concerts, dances, etc. can make a valuable anchor for recall. The technique sounds deceptively simple but actually can require considerable finesse. Frequent summarizing, repetitions of the purpose of the assessments, and expressions of empathy for the difficulty of recall can make the process markedly more productive.

3.3.1   Encouraging Assessment

Some clients, often for multiple reasons, resist the assessment process. Many think that this sort of dwelling on the past will prove counterproductive. Reflecting these opinions often reveals a great deal of negative affect associated with past behaviors, which can be a very therapeutic interaction. In addition, clinicians can explain that thorough information on patterns of use makes interventions easier. A keen understanding of the amount, frequency, and circumstances of use can help clients monitor their progress. Clients also claim that they will be unable to recall exact amounts, but if they are willing to start with the current date and work backwards, they are often surprised at how well they remember. Even the most resistant clients can state if they have used on the current day, and it's a gentle leap to the day before and the day before that. This gradual working backward soon leads to a potentially difficult but exceptionally useful 90-day assessment. Starting with a calendar page showing the current month is usually a welcome approach. Mark any key dates of special events. Recurring events like paydays, regular meetings, workdays, or weekends are worth marking, too. Moving backwards from the current day is easiest for most clients. Beginning with questions about that particular day works wonders. As odd as it sounds, "Do you remember that day?" can get

Clinical Pearl
Recalling Quantities of Drugs Consumed

The recall of quantities, especially for some illicit drugs, can get complicated. Any unit of measurement that appeals to the client is usually best. Cannabis users have reported bowls, blunts, grams, joints, and even bong hits. Crack cocaine users often conceptualize quantity in terms of dollar amounts. Intranasal cocaine users frequently remember amounts in grams. Users of prescription drugs often recall the number of pills they took. Almost invariably, clients reach a certain day and claim that the amount was tremendously large but impossible to recall. Responses like "I don't know, but it was a lot," can actually be a great place to start. Comparing that day to other days with large amounts often helps jog their memories. Mentioning an absurdly large amount can often help clients move towards a reasonable estimate. "Do you think you snorted 4 grams?" can help clients overcome any embarrassment they might have about snorting 2 grams. Questions like "Was it more than on the 24th?" can help clients put the day's use in perspective relative to other sessions of use. Throwing out a range of responses comparable to those reported from other days can also help. Questions like "Do you think it was more than $700 worth?" or "Was it more than 4 pills?" can start a series of questions moving higher and lower to get a good estimate of consumption. Precise estimates of quantity can prove particularly important as clients make progress toward recovery.

people started. Asking if they drank alcohol that day and, if so, how much, can lead into the use of other drugs. Whether they used or not is important, but information about the quantity of use will also be helpful later in treatment.

Many clients initially claim a specific, invariable pattern but later realize that their use ranges more than they thought. Those who say that they drink a six-pack and take four painkillers each night are often surprised when they walk through individual days and discover that, for example, weekdays they use markedly less and weekends they use considerably more than their average. This type of variation will actually prove useful when planning for high-risk situations later in treatment. This assessment also lays the groundwork for a functional analysis of the predictors, correlates, and consequences of use, as detailed in Section 4.

Assessments can enhance the therapeutic relationship as well as provide data

An important but untouted bonus of the Timeline Follow-Back or any interview is its potential for the development of a good therapeutic relationship. The recall of each day's use should focus as much as possible on different drugs and their amounts. However, it can be counterproductive to sacrifice rapport simply to get precise data. If a client recalls that a specific date marked a negative life event, express empathy and support before moving to the next date. Any client could lose heart when the pursuit of exact amounts grows too persistent. After revealing that a day marked the death of a parent or the initiation of a divorce, few would like the therapist's first response to be "And did you snort cocaine that day?" Acknowledging that these events must have been difficult can encourage a candid assessment of use and builds good connections between client and therapist.

Figure 3
Example Timeline Follow Back

	Sunday	Monday	Tuesday	Wednesday	Thursday	Friday	Saturday
February							
	1	2-Groundhog Day	3	4	5	6	7
	1 gram pot	0.5 gram pot	0.5 gram pot	0.5 gram pot	0.5 gram pot	1 gram pot	1 gram pot
	4 drinks	3 drinks	4 drinks	5 drinks	6 drinks	0.5 gram cocaine	1 gram cocaine
						6 drinks	6 drinks
	8	9	10	11	12-Lincoln's Birthday	13	14-St. Valentine's Day
	1 gram pot	0.5 gram pot	0.5 gram pot	0.5 gram pot	0.5 gram pot	1 gram pot	1 gram pot
	4 drinks	2 drinks	2 drinks	3 drinks	5 drinks	0.5 gram cocaine	1 gram cocaine
						5 drinks	8 drinks
	15	16-President's Day	17	18	19	20	21
	1 gram pot	3 drinks	3 drinks	3 drinks	4 drinks	3 drinks	4 drinks
	4 drinks	8 Vicodin	8 Vicodin	8 Vicodin	10 Vicodin	12 Vicodin	12 Vicodin
	8 Vicodin						
	22-Washington's Birthday	23	24	25-Ash Wednesday	26	27	28
	1 gram pot	4 Ritalin	4 Ritalin	4 Ritalin	0.5 gram pot	1 gram pot	1 gram pot
	4 drinks				0.5 gram cocaine	1 gram cocaine	1 gram cocaine
					4 drinks	4 drinks	5 drinks

3.4   The Inventory of Drug Use Consequences (InDUC)

In contrast to the TLFB, which is an interview that focuses on use, the InDUC is a self-report questionnaire that concentrates on negative consequences of drug use in a variety of domains. This type of self-administered paper-and-pencil questionnaire can prove convenient and helpful if clients get the chance to review and discuss answers as part of the assessment process. In contrast, completing the scale regularly without comments or questions can lead clients to take the questionnaire less seriously. Self-report questionnaires can be great tools for research but they will only help clinical work if therapists communicate their importance.

The recent and lifetime versions of the InDUC focus on different periods, allowing for the assessment of changes as treatment continues. The recent version can serve as a nice index of progress after several sessions of treatment, helping clients detail the domains where they have improved. The full scale contains 50 yes/no items that tap negative consequences in five domains: physical, interpersonal, intrapersonal, impulse control, and social responsibility (Tonigan & Miller, 2002). The physical subscale asks questions about health, physical appearance, sexual dysfunction, and troubled sleep. The interpersonal items focus on family relationships, parenting, and friendships. The intrapersonal scale examines personality, personal growth, and spiritual or moral aspects of life. The impulse control scale focuses on risky behaviors related to drug use. The social responsibility items assess work, school, and social functioning. Although the full scale is typically not burdensome, a brief version (15 items) is also available. The multiple domains of negative consequences can provide a focus for treatment when clients contemplate changing their drug use. Therapists can devote extra time to domains where the negative consequences are more prevalent or severe.

The questionnaire also contains control items designed to identify minimizing, infrequency, or inattentiveness. These items ask questions that nearly everyone with drug-related problems would have to endorse, such as "I have enjoyed drinking or using drugs". Clients with many "no" responses to these items should get the chance to explain their answers in session (see http://casaa.unm.edu/inst/InDUC-2L-SOm.pdf, and the Appendix in this book).

3.5   Motivation to Change

Motivation remains a consistently complex and useful predictor of treatment outcome. Measuring motivation is now an important aspect of many health-related interventions and investigations (Walters, Rotgers, Saunders, Wilkonson, & Towers, 2003). Researchers have developed several measures of motivation. These include the Stage of Change Readiness and Treatment Eagerness Scale (SOCRATES; Miller & Tonigan, 1997, the University of Rhode Island Change Assessment (URICA; McConnaughy, Prochaska, & Velicer, 1983), and the Readiness to Change Questionnaire (RTCQ; Rollnick, Heather, Gold, & Hall, 1992). These measures contain from a dozen to over 30

On the ruler below, please circle the number that best describes how you feel *right now*:

1	2	3	4	5	6	7	8	9	10

I never think about changing my drug use.	Sometimes I think about changing my drug use.	I have decided to change my drug use.	I am already trying to change my drugs.	I have changed my drug use and use less than before.

Figure 4
Motivation to Change Ruler

items and attempt to determine the level of motivation of individuals by placing them in the appropriate level of the change continuum. Practitioners often need an assessment of readiness to change that can provide a quick measure of who would benefit most from treatment or who has made progress in increasing their motivation. The *contemplation ladder* or *ruler,* developed originally for smoking cessation by Biener and Abrams (1991), is a brief and affordable assessment tool that correlates highly with longer questionnaires (see Figure 4). These rulers show good discriminant validity across different behaviors. For example, a ruler that asks about motivation to change binge drinking correlated over 0.7 with the RTCQ for the same behavior, but less than 0.2 with a ruler addressing safer sex (LaBrie, Quinlan, Schifffman, & Earleywine, 2005).

3.6   Treatment History

Client reports on previous treatments can reveal a great deal about motivation, expectations and goals. The number of previous treatment attempts, both formal and informal, can be an excellent place to start. Information on the modality of treatment, whether inpatient, outpatient, or residential, can help inform decisions about current therapy. Getting a feel for the client's understanding of the previous treatment approaches also can reveal a lot. Some clients miss essential components of treatment the first time through for reasons ranging from distracting withdrawal symptoms, inadequate recovery of cognitive functioning, or a lack of readiness to change at the time. Clients may feel that prior therapy genuinely worked for them but simply needs some fine-tuning to get them back on track. Others may have found previous approaches unacceptable for a variety of reasons, or they have somehow habituated to these approaches and need to return to the central ideas presented in a different way. These reactions can help the client and clinician choose alternatives that are more acceptable.

Changing problem drug use often requires multiple attempts

Interpreting this information can prove difficult. It is hard to know if a return to treatment after previous attempts reflects a great deal of motivation or very little. One approach to the problem involves sharing the dilemma with the client. The statement: "Some clients come back to treatment time and again because they are motivated; others because they aren't" can initiate this conversation. It also makes a nice transition to assessments of motivation to change. It's important to avoid framing these previous treatments as failures. Any major behavior change can require multiple attempts (Prochaska & DiClemente, 2005). Prior treatments may have provided the essential information and experience to make the current attempt a complete success. If clinicians view these previous treatments as part of a larger self-change process that the client can build upon in the current therapy, the chances of feeling demoralized about a return to treatment can decrease. Open-ended questions like, "What do you make of your treatment up to now?" and "How can we add to your previous progress?" can encourage clients to view change as ongoing while they reveal their attitudes, beliefs, and experiences about previous therapy.

3.7　Social Support

Few clients enter treatment as an island, isolated from all other people, and the importance of social support in substance abuse treatment outcome is well-documented (Warren, Stein, & Grella, 2007). Some members of the client's social network will prove more helpful to changes in behavior than others. Thorough assessments of all the potential people in a client's circle often reveal markedly larger numbers of supports than the client may initially identify. Candid discussions of spouses, partners, grandparents, parents, children, grandchildren, siblings, friends, coworkers, and acquaintances can provide a sense for who might support change and who might undermine it. Therapists can benefit from knowing which of these people use drugs and in what ways. The clients' impressions of each person's likely reaction to behavior change can inform decisions about who is and is not an ideal associate, particularly in the beginning of this process. Interpretations of social support invariably rest on assumptions. Personal feelings about independence and intimacy are ideographic. One person's idea of closeness could sound smothering to another. The clients' perception of which people are most available and skilled for soothing, providing instrumental support, and encouraging drug-free socializing will also prove informative.

Two terms from the twelve-step literature that frequently appear in discussions of social support are enabling and codependence. Generally, *enabling* refers to behaviors that allow substance users to escape the negative consequences of their actions. Calling a spouse's office to claim he is sick when he is actually recovering from a binge is considered enabling. *Codependence* usually refers to people whose primary relationships are with problem substance users who require considerable enabling. It is not a formal diagnosis and its discriminant validity with established disorders is questionable. Despite their potential intuitive appeal, neither of these terms has much empirical support. They are also laden with connotations that vary dramatically from person to person, potentially confusing or alienating clients. Nevertheless, the idea that some people in a drug user's social network will encourage actions that may lead to trouble resonates with most clients. Identifying who is most likely in the long run to support new behaviors rather than old ones can prove particularly helpful.

Methods of Treatment

4.1   Overview

Empirically validated approaches to treatment have the potential to create dramatic change very rapidly; some studies suggest even a single session can alter drug use significantly. Therapists who approach intervention with the idea that people can improve quickly are more likely to communicate this possibility to clients. They also have data on their side. Nevertheless, many clients require more time than some treatment outcome studies imply, and there is no need to rush. Clients rarely develop drug problems overnight. It follows that changing these problems can sometimes take several sessions. An adept clinician can encourage regular attendance and adherence to a treatment plan by staying flexible and adjusting therapy to the needs of the client. Once clients change problematic drug use, they are often interested in remaining in treatment to address other interesting aspects of optimal functioning. Clinicians can make superb use of their time by focusing on the key components of therapies that have documented improvement, the empirically supported treatments (ESTs).

4.1.1   Empirically supported treatments (ESTs)

Manualized therapy leads to better outcomes than a placebo or waiting list when conducted with a well-described client population (Tryon & Misurell, 2008). In an era in which managed care demands documented improvement, ESTs offer assurance that the therapy can help a specific disorder in a specific group. Many ESTs are relatively brief, suggesting that they provide efficient alleviation of symptoms. Using treatments that have proven effective has ethical and economic advantages as well. Nevertheless, the recent wave of enthusiasm for ESTs is not without criticism. Meta-analyses of treatment outcome studies have shown that no single effective treatment is appreciably better than another (Wampold, et al., 1997). Nevertheless, these results do not suggest that any approach will work. Unfortunately, some critics of ESTs interpret this outcome as a justification to stick with approaches that are not supported by the research literature.

Empirical validation is no guarantee that a particular treatment is optimal, particularly for a specific client under specific circumstances. Empirical validation is often derived from large research studies lacking representative client diversity, both in problem presentation and background. This predicament raises concerns regarding the optimal treatment for the client sitting in the office today. Nevertheless, even if research outcomes do not address all the needs of a particular client, the principles and techniques employed will likely help.

Treatments that help enhance motivation to change, improve coping, increase a client's ability to manage negative moods, provide better problem-solving skills, develop supportive interpersonal relationships, and train clients to find rewarding alternative behaviors lead to the best outcomes. Sufficient duration of treatment can also be important. Contrary to classical notions, an appreciation for a sufficient duration of treatment does not necessarily translate to a large number of sessions, but rather to an appropriate amount of time to allow for change. For example, a four-session treatment for cannabis problems led to better outcomes when delivered over three months than when delivered over one month (Jungerman, Andreoni, & Laranjeira, 2007). Allowing sufficient time for contemplation and practice may enhance therapy even without lengthening the number or duration of sessions. Clinicians who focus on the aspects of treatment mentioned here can rest assured that they are helping.

4.1.2   Harm Reduction, Drug Safety, and Abstinence

It's easier to track progress with a definite goal in mind. For substance abusing clients, the goal may seem obvious at first glance, but grows complicated upon further inspection. Abstinence goals have a great deal of intuitive appeal. Drugs are certainly unlikely to create problems for people who do not use them. Treatment traditions, particularly in the US, highlight addiction as a disease that requires complete abstinence from all intoxicants (see Marlatt, 2002). Proponents of this abstinence approach emphasize how exposure to drug cues and intoxication of any sort increases the risk for relapse and subsequent problems. Some treatment providers view the desire to continue drug use as a form of denial or a set of cognitions that will likely interfere with long-term change. They see any attempts to train clients to use drugs in less harmful ways as enabling or otherwise impairing progress.

Abstaining from drugs completely is an admirable goal. Nevertheless, some people use drugs without developing negative consequences. Working with a client who longs to alter drug use but not eliminate it can put clinicians in a quandary about ethics, liability, and a good treatment approach. Many drug users who recover naturally from problems simply limit their consumption without abstaining completely (Klingemann & Sobell, 2007; Sobell, Ellingstad, & Sobell, 2000). Some who attend abstinence-based treatments even show improvement without maintaining abstinence (see Sobell & Sobell, 2000). A variety of factors and circumstances unrelated to drugs can contribute to problematic drug use. Many clients experience problems that they view as independent of their drug use. Others identify negative consequences of taking drugs but do not want to set a goal of total abstinence. Entertaining alternative goals might help keep clients in treatment who might leave under other circumstances. Clients who do not have an abstinence goal can still benefit from treatment (Adamson & Sellman, 2001; King & Tucker, 2000).

Harm Reduction Goals
One of the biggest advantages of entertaining alternatives to abstinence in the initial stages of treatment is the opportunity to engage more clients in therapy.

Many who desire to change their drug use find that treatments devoted to abstinence do not fit their goals, so they never attend therapy or drop out early in the process (Marlatt, 2002). Clients who leave treatment cannot benefit from it. Clinicians who consider alternative goals carefully can communicate a collaborative spirit and build rapport. They also plant the seed for the option of abstinence. Clients who entered treatment for problems that they did not view as drug-related could balk at the notion of complete abstinence, but assessment might convince them that altering use could provide important benefits.

Anxiety-ridden clients who coincidentally consume 11 cups of coffee per day may not initially recognize the link between their symptoms and drug use. Accordingly, they may be incredibly reluctant to abandon a habit that they perceive as a source of productivity, but would likely prove willing to decrease consumption in the hope of alleviating symptoms. The daily marijuana smoker who suffers from fatigue and malaise might consider altering the timing, frequency, and quantity of use before contemplating refraining entirely. Clients who have no symptoms of dependence or abuse but find themselves with other drug-related problems may be markedly more willing to discuss decreased drug consumption than complete abstinence. Flexibility about goals for treatment has the potential to decrease problems even when abstinence is not the client's stated preference or desire.

It is important to recognize that those who enter treatment with drug problems in mind have often made their very best attempts to solve their problems on their own. These attempts often do not include multi-faceted strategies for decreasing stress, managing emotions, or learning new interpersonal skills. Many clients report simply trying to use less often or in smaller amounts but without any alteration in daily activities, leisure, or other aspects of life that might make decreased use easier. In a sense, they do not alter psychological, social, or biological contributors to their use, so altering use proves difficult. A careful assessment of these previous attempts can help determine if abstinence is essential. Those who have experienced extreme negative consequences, marked symptoms of dependence, and frequent relapses may decide that abstinence seems the most appropriate goal. Those who are unwilling to try abstinence first can still benefit from treatment. Turning to safer drugs, modifying modes of administration, changing the times of use, and finding alternative activities that provide comparable benefits can help. Permitting clients to make these attempts will either lead them to moderate consumption and minimize problems or strengthen the case for abstinence as a goal (Denning, 2004).

Decreasing Quantity and Frequency

An obvious strategy for minimizing drug-related harm involves using drugs less often and in smaller amounts. This approach alone can be a difficult one. A candid discussion about appropriate quantities and frequencies of use can reveal unrealistic or wishful client expectations about the risk of exceeding specified goals or developing negative consequences. Although the goal of using less can be an admirable one, it is difficult to achieve without detailed plans. Frank assessments of previous attempts to change behavior can help clients recognize when amounts or frequencies were excessive in the past, potentially leading to more realistic ideas about acceptable levels of use. These

Harm reduction strategies may attract clients who might resist abstinence goals

discussions may actually motivate further consideration of abstinence. As a cocaine-using client once said, "If I can't have an eight ball, what's the point?" In truth, if the client's history of use shows consistent, troublesome binges, a discussion of controlled use can reveal that abstinence may actually be the most appropriate goal for treatment.

Using Alternative Substances

The idea of turning to safer drugs is particularly controversial, but some substances are markedly safer than others (see Denning, Little, & Glickman, 2004). A client once put the idea best after he was teased for his copious use of coffee and cigarettes at AA meetings: "Coffee and cigarettes never made me wake up broke and naked." Generally, expert ratings on addictiveness or physical harm are highest for heroin and cocaine and lowest for cannabis, caffeine, and hallucinogens (Gore & Earleywine, 2007; Nutt, King, Saulsbury, & Blakemore, 2007). Using drugs associated with fewer negative consequences can be a positive step toward eliminating problems. Clients who are unwilling to consider a drug-free lifestyle might abstain from the most dangerous drugs like heroin and cocaine but continue to use cannabis and the occasional hallucinogen. Cannabis has the potential for dependence but rarely produces the negative consequences of heroin or cocaine, has less severe legal penalties, and may ease withdrawal from other drugs. The cannabis vaporizer, which heats the plant material without lighting it on fire, may decrease the chances of respiratory irritation. Edible forms of cannabis will not create pulmonary problems. In some individuals, cannabis intoxication may reduce resolutions to avoid harder drugs. Clients who cannot refrain from using other drugs under these circumstances should receive clear feedback about the potential benefits of contingency plans or abstinence.

Choosing Different Strategies of Administration

Altering the patterns of administration can also improve drug safety. Again, this strategy generates controversy, but several changes in drug administration decrease the risk of problems. Generally, avoiding simultaneous polydrug use, choosing safer techniques for ingesting the drugs, understanding signs of overdose, and altering the time of day of administration can decrease negative outcomes. Details of these strategies appear below.

Avoiding Simultaneous Polydrug Use

Refraining from mixing psychoactive substances can be an important first step toward reducing negative consequences. Drugs can become dramatically more toxic when mixed with other drugs. For example, the amount of barbiturates required for a lethal dose drops significantly if alcohol is also consumed. Consuming cocaine and alcohol creates a novel chemical with very different properties (cocaethylene) that does not appear if either drug is consumed alone. Even over-the-counter drugs with few psychoactive effects can alter responses to drugs of abuse. For example, antihistamines seem to increase the impact of opiates. Safe decisions about dosage, method, and timing of use of still more opiates become more difficult during intoxication, particularly if the intoxication is larger because of the ingestion of antihistamines. Clients often reveal that some of their most aversive experiences with drugs arise when they consume them in combination. Educating clients on the increased probability of negative outcomes when drugs are mixed can be time well spent.

Choosing Safer Methods of Drug Administration

The technique for bringing the drug into the body has a dramatic impact on its effect and associated problems. Intravenous administration has incredible risks for complications of all sorts. Injections carry the risk of necrotizing fasciitis (flesh-eating bacteria), botulism, and tetanus (lockjaw). Those who insist on injection sometimes turn to subcutaneous (under the skin; also known as "skin popping") injection, which has the potential to decrease risk for overdose, but may increase risks of various infections. Anyone injecting drugs should understand appropriate injection procedures that minimize harm. Frank discussions on this topic actually can underline the dangers of injection and may help encourage clients to turn to alternative forms of drug administration. Injection requires a clean syringe to avoid blood-borne illnesses like hepatitis and AIDS. To minimize some complications, injectors should change injection sites for each shot, always clean the site with alcohol, use the smallest needle possible, and never inject into red or sore tissue. Injectors should avoid crushing pills to inject because of the many types of fillers that they contain that are incompatible with safe injection. Good injection techniques decrease the risk of abscesses and the collections of pus that accumulate in cavities formed in infected tissue. It is not, however, a guarantee of problem-free use.

Details about AIDS, hepatitis, flesh-eating bacteria, infected cavities filled with pus, and death might inspire a discussion of alternative routes of administration. Smoked versions of many injected drugs provide comparable effects without the risks associated with needles. Providing clients who inject heroin with foil for smoking it has shown promise for reducing harm in this group (Pizzey & Hunt, 2008). Smoking is not without its risks, of course, as the possibility of lung irritation and other respiratory troubles, as well as continued dependence, remains. Insufflated (snorted) versions may lack the rapid onset of effects but also minimizes the chances of problems associated with injection or smoking, as long as users do not share straws. Those who choose to snort drugs can decrease nasal irritation with a saline spray or by snorting a small amount of water before and after the drug. These complications pale in comparison to hepatitis or AIDS, but smoked and insufflated drugs remain highly addictive and can still result in an overdose. These techniques cannot eliminate all the potential problems of substance dependence. Details about these strategies appear in brief handouts available on-line from the Harm Reduction Coalition (www.harmreduction.org).

Understanding Overdose

All opiate users, but particularly injectors, should know the signs of overdose and train their friends to recognize them as well. Loss of consciousness demands an intervention. Overdose typically causes a limp body, inability to speak, slow breathing, blue tinge in lips or nails, choking or gurgling sounds, and vomiting. Opiate users should have NARCAN, an opiate antagonist, handy to avoid potentially fatal consequences of an overdose. NARCAN is available as a nasal spray that heroin users express a willingness to administer to peers (Kerr, Dietze, Kelly, & Jolley, 2008). Most harm reduction centers will provide it free of charge. Many of these centers appear on the internet at http://www.harmreductiontherapy.org. Overdosing on stimulants has dramatically different symptoms: chest pain, difficulty breathing, ringing in the ears, headache, rapid heartbeat, sweating, and shaking. A call to emergency services can be essential in these situations. Stimulant overdoses are frequently fatal. A simple rule for stimulant users that is common in harm-reduction therapy can make these overdoses unlikely: Never take an additional dose of a stimulant without recovering completely from the first. Adhering to harm reduction goals will make overdoses unlikely. Frank discussions of these symptoms and the severity of the problems that they can generate emphasize the importance of sticking to these goals. These discussions may also pave the way for reconsidering abstinence goals.

Varying Time of Administration

Although research on the time of administration of drugs is in its infancy, the timing of use tends to covary with problems (Denning et al., 2004; Gallerani et al., 2001). Key factors include getting high at inappropriate times and administering subsequent doses while high. Using drugs only when important obligations are not impending certainly decreases the risk of negative consequences when compared to getting high immediately prior to work, school, or childcare duties. Clients who are willing to plan use to avoid intoxication at inappropriate times have markedly better chances for decreasing problems. In addition, using a small amount of a drug and refraining from subsequent doses during intoxication can decrease the probability of ill-advised continuations of use or problematic behaviors that might arise from impaired judgment.

Protective Behaviors

A rich literature has developed on techniques and strategies that decrease the negative consequences of alcohol consumption (e.g., Martens, Pederson, LaBrie, Ferrier, & Cimini, 2007); many of these apply to other drugs as well. Some focus on decreasing quantities. These include various strategies for tracking and limiting consumption. Users can set a predetermined limit on the quantity they will consume in a given session, monitor the amount consumed, ask friends to assist them in monitoring, stop use at a predetermined time, and pace their consumption over a session to keep quantities limited. Other strategies focus on expense as well as quantity, where users set a predetermined amount of money aside to spend. They do not carry cash or ask for credit to purchase more drugs.

Dealing with an underground market requires its own set of associated protective behaviors. These include only purchasing from familiar people in safe settings, purchasing small amounts that have less severe legal consequences for possession, and never selling drugs. Other protective behaviors focus on aspects of the environment rather than the quantity consumed. These include using a designated driver, only using drugs in safe environs, and limiting consumption to moments when sufficient free time is available to recover from effects before other obligations begin.

Clinical Pearl
Harm Reduction

A marijuana user presents for treatment who reports coughing and wheezing despite no use of cigarettes, a wife who feels disconnected from him because of frequent periods of "spaciness," and a general lack of leisure skills and activities. He reports no symptoms of abuse and only a single symptom of dependence – reduced activities. He is not interested in an abstinence goal. He initially suggests that he only gets high a couple of times per week.

The TLFB reveals that he smokes two joints per day on four days per week. Feedback about use leads to a discussion of what would be acceptable. He chooses to smoke one gram or less on two occasions per week. Discussion of his wife's complaints reveals that on weekends he tends to get high first thing in the morning. He agrees that this habit contributes to her perception of frequent "spaciness" as well as his decrease in activities. He decides that he should not get high before 7 p.m. He is uninformed about the vaporizer but is willing to purchase one in an effort to reduce respiratory symptoms. Over subsequent weeks, he reports decreasing use successfully, with marked decreases in respiratory symptoms and complaints from his spouse. He also mentions a renewed interest in reading for pleasure.

This new arrangement may be less than ideal in the minds of many clinicians, but provides an opportunity for continued monitoring of negative consequences, engages a client who might otherwise be uninterested in an intervention, and sets the groundwork for discussions of an abstinence goal if the current arrangement fails.

4.2 Efficacy and Prognosis

The efficacy of substance abuse treatment can depend upon duration of treatment, the drug of choice, route of administration, and numerous other factors. Different drugs appear to have different trajectories of use across the lifespan (Hser, Longshore, & Anglin, 2007). Among problem users, marijuana and methamphetamine use often decreases with time from the teen years onward. Cocaine use often increases into late 20s and early 30s but then declines. In contrast, heroin use often increases with age, at least in recent cohorts. Users show nearly every possible pattern of use trajectories, with early cessation a genuine possibility and a desirable outcome. Periods of abstinence, lapses, and relapses are common. Some users consume drugs often and in large amounts but gradually decrease use over years. Others use heavily and consistently, some for decades. Key life events, including marriage, incarceration, parenthood, and treatment can have dramatic impacts on a drug user's trajectory.

Current treatment approaches that focus on brief interventions can seem to imply that drug dependence parallels other acute conditions. Nevertheless, drug problems can persist, much like a chronic illness. Brief interventions undoubtedly can help users achieve abstinence, but keeping lapses and relapses to a minimum may require frequent and consistent follow-ups. Data on the transition from initiation to problematic use suggest that frank discussions with recreational users who do not view their use as problematic can also help

Drug problems can persist like a chronic illness

minimize complications. The average time from initiation of drug use to first treatment can range dramatically, often 5–10 years. An important subset of individuals recovers from some drug problems with little or no intervention and few subsequent troubles (Sobell at al., 2000). Others, however, have more difficulty. Among heroin users, the quest for stable recovery can run from 8 to 10 years (Hser et al., 2007).

The course of drug dependence can prove long and complex. Negative consequences of use are likely. Outcomes are worse for drug-involved individuals than comparable people who do not use illicit drugs. For example, a 20-year follow-up of opiate addicts revealed that they had higher mortality rates than the average nonusing person over the elapsed period (Bjornaas et al., 2008). The addicts had higher rates of death for all causes, but accidents, suicide, and complications of drug use were particularly common.

Route of administration can also prove important in predicting prognosis and course. Smoked and injected drugs reach the brain quickly, creating abrupt changes in subjective experience that appear more reinforcing than the same drugs taken in ways that create a more gradual onset of effects (Julien, 2005). Administering drugs in ways that lead to a rapid and dramatic onset of effects often leads to greater problems. For example, methamphetamine users can have markedly different outcomes depending on whether they inject the drug, smoke it, or use it intranasally. Injectors experienced more use during treatment, worse treatment outcomes, and more psychological and medical problems than people who used methamphetamine intranasally. Those who smoked methamphetamine also experienced greater negative consequences. The quest for a "rush" or "quick buzz" may indicate a greater propensity for problems. In addition, the physiological experience of speedy, drug-induced changes may increase the probability for negative consequences (Rawson, Gonzales, Marinelli-Casey, & Ang, 2007).

4.3   The Therapeutic Relationship as a Mechanism of Action

The mechanisms underlying these effective treatments fit within the biopsychosocial model. Generally, the psychotherapies rely on social interaction to enhance motivation, alter cognitions, and improve skills to decrease the negative consequences of drugs. Pharmacotherapies tend to decrease craving or alter responses to drugs to help achieve the same goal. The fact that multiple approaches achieve the same ends may arise because of nonspecific factors in treatment.

Warmth, empathy, and genuineness can help the therapeutic relationship

Almost all psychotherapies rely on general principles to help clients decrease problems. The therapist behaves in ways that increase the likelihood of improvement. These behaviors, the nonspecifics of change, likely play a large role in treatment outcome. The general behaviors most likely to induce change in a social interaction involve empathy, nonpossessive warmth, and genuineness. Carl Rogers emphasized these attributes in the treatment he invented, client-centered therapy (Rogers, 1951). These therapist actions appear in successful treatments of all sorts. The presence of these behaviors in many treatments may serve as a good explanation for why different thera-pies produce comparable results (Wampold et al., 1997). A healing relation-ship with a nonjudgmental, attentive, directive person can facilitate change independently of a therapist's claimed theoretical orientation. This empathy, warmth, and genuineness lay the foundation for any productive, therapeutic interaction. Many therapies rely on these aspects of the relationship to help support both problem reduction and client growth.

4.3.1 Empathy

Although many people have an implicit feel for empathy, nonpossessive warmth, and genuineness, these qualities prove difficult to define in the abstract. Empathy concerns the ability to identify with another person's feel-ings. Empathic reactions clearly indicate that the therapist understands the client's view of situations, without implying that the therapist knows exactly what it's like to be that person. In addition, empathic therapists appear moti-vated to understand what clients mean as well as what they say. This under-standing and empathy have great importance in the treatment of substance abuse. Therapists may have never experienced each client's situation exactly, but they are certainly familiar with frustration, disappointment, sadness, and the range of emotions that accompany change. Expressions of this empathy enhance the relationship between client and therapist. This sharing of feel-ing may increase the client's trust, encouraging candid disclosures. Sorting through the ambivalent and conflicted feelings associated with drug problems may help clients make clear decisions about decreasing the negative conse-quences of their use. Even among clinicians who use comparable or identi-cal treatment approaches, empathy can predict outcome quite well (Miller, 2000). A great deal of the communication of empathy involves reflection, as discussed below.

4.3.2 Warmth

Nonpossessive warmth refers to a therapist's interactive style. Warmth sug-gests a generally good-natured approach to therapy, and a sincere appreciation of the client's situation. The nonpossessive aspect implies that the therapist does not withdraw warmth if clients have lapses of some sort. The warmth does not disappear and reappear with changes in behavior. Thus, clients need not fear a bad reaction if they report emotions or behaviors they consider negative. The therapist's style should not change if the client grows upset, reports urges, or uses drugs. Many substance users have never experienced a relationship that includes nonpossessive warmth. Demonstrations of warmth vary among therapists as they do among other people. Nevertheless, a sincere smile, an attentive nod, and considerate listening invariably enhance interac-tions and reveal warmth. Any therapist who mentions that a session has gone well or praises a client for attempts at change can appear warm.

4.3.3 Genuineness

Genuineness arises from authentic, trustworthy, realistic behaviors that are consistent with the therapist's attitudes, values, and goals. Clients rely on sincere reactions that are free from affectation or pretense. A therapist who seems natural creates a more comfortable atmosphere than one who appears scripted, stilted, or phony. Therapists who show genuineness have body language, eye contact, and facial expressions that correspond to their words. Essentially, the human interaction should feel more important than taking notes or following a treatment protocol. This quality enhances rapport. Clients of therapists who show genuine interactions report feeling that they are getting to know the therapist, in the sense that they relate to each other rather than simply exchange information. Although it's hard to point to specific actions out of context and label them genuine or not, people easily identify therapists who seem consistent, true to themselves, and real (Miller & Rollnick, 2002). Research suggests that these therapists can produce better outcomes than other therapists performing the same type of therapy.

Unfortunately, the results of this research are occasionally misinterpreted to mean that any treatment is good as long as the therapist and client have a good relationship. A warm, empathic, genuine relationship is an essential foundation for therapy, but probably not enough to alter problematic drug use as efficiently as possible. Specific techniques that go beyond the therapeutic relationship can improve overall outcomes. They can also enhance the rate of change in problem behaviors.

4.4 Combinations of Methods

The psychological treatments that have received empirical support for drug abuse and dependence include motivational interviewing, cognitive-behavioral therapy, 12-step facilitation, contingency management, brief strategic family therapy, multidimensional family therapy, and psychodynamic (supportive-expressive) therapy. An in-depth review of each of these approaches is beyond the scope of this book. Instead, details on a combination of motivational interviewing and cognitive behavioral techniques appear; this combination is consistent with the highly successful Guided Self-Change approach (Sobell & Sobell, 1998, 2005; Sobell, Wagner, Sobell, Agrawal, & Ellingstad, 2006), which has proven successful in helping people with various addictive problems. Given the ubiquitous nature of 12-step programs (Carrico, Gifford, & Moos, 2007), a general overview of this approach appears as well. In addition, pharmacological adjuncts to treatment are described to give clinicians a general feel for these approaches.

4.4.1 Motivational Interviewing

Motivational interviewing (Miller & Rollnick, 2002) relies on brief interactions with a therapist to help clients decrease problems. The treatment enhances motivation before attempting any changes in behavior. Therapists adopt this approach because any efforts to teach techniques for limiting drug use are a waste of time if clients are unmotivated to apply them. Once a client's motivation has increased, strategies for eliminating drug problems have a better chance of success. Motivational interviewing focuses on identifying the client's own reasons to quit. Once these reasons help increase desire, clients often develop their own strategies for eliminating problem drug use.

Many people stop using drugs on their own; motivational interviewing essentially enhances the chances that a client will join this group. The social interaction with the therapist may highlight the negative consequences of drug use and support clients' feelings that they can make progress, leading people to change their own lives. Developing competence in motivational interviewing requires markedly more than reading a few pages. A comprehensive collection of resources on this topic and opportunities for training appear at www.motivationalinterview.org. The following pages can give clinicians a general feel for the process and techniques.

The Spirit of Motivational Interviewing

The spirit of motivational interviewing rests on the warmth, empathy, and genuineness discussed in the section on nonspecifics of therapy. The originators of the treatment consistently emphasize that it is *collaborative* – a unique solution designed by the client with input from the therapist. The treatment is both client centered and directive, which may seem impossible at first glance. It is client centered in the sense that the clients are viewed as experts on their own history, desires, aims, and reactions. It is directive in the sense that the clinician continually returns discussion to the disparity between client values and problem behaviors in an effort to facilitate a better life.

Although motivational interviewing is not a set of techniques so much as a way of being with clients that can enhance their motivation to change themselves, specific strategies and procedures that are consistent with the treatment's overarching principles make sessions productive. The treatment tends to create change through several steps. The clinician provides clients with feedback about their drug use and its consequences in a nonjudgmental way. The therapist then lets the client hash out the understandable concerns about changing drug use while showing warmth and support. The therapist sticks to the client's agenda and concerns but asks questions and makes comments in a way that will elicit talk of changing the behavior. Once the client has decided to change, the therapist explores options with the client to design a strategy that is consistent with stated goals and appears likely to succeed.

At least four general principles underlie the spirit of motivational interviewing: express empathy, develop discrepancy, roll with resistance, and support self-efficacy.

Express empathy

As mentioned, expressing empathy is consistent with reflective listening skills, also known as accurate empathy. Reflective listening has developed a curious reputation ever since Joseph Weizenbaum's notorious ELIZA program (Weizenbaum, 1966) parodied nondirective therapists by rewording "client" input as questions in a way that mimicked the therapy process. This program required a user to enter a sentence; it then spit the essential information back as a question. The generated conversations sounded hauntingly like therapy performed by a fatigued, overworked clinician functioning on automatic pilot. Clearly, genuine reflections require more.

In fact, some of the best reflections are not questions but statements that communicate an understanding of what the client has said. Using statements instead of questions allows clients to continue the discussion on that same topic or move to another. A reflection statement allows clients to elaborate if they choose, but they can change to a new topic as they progress. In contrast to statements, therapist questions can steer the conversation in a direction that is less important to the client. Thus, reflections worded as statements can prove more productive in the long run. These simple reflections that rephrase the client's own words as a statement have their place in expressing empathy, but other levels of reflection are potentially more important. In particular, rephrasing, reflecting feeling, and using agreement with a twist are important techniques for communicating acceptance and encouraging change.

Clinical Pearl
Reflection

Simple reflections, rephrasing, reflecting feeling, agreement with a twist, and double-sided reflections can all communicate empathy, keep discussions of change rolling, and help clients explore their feelings about drug use and consequences.

Simple reflections. Simple reflections, as the name suggests, state clients' words back to them, communicating that the therapist has heard and understands. They keep conversation flowing and allow clients to elaborate or change to another topic as they see fit. A client may state, "I don't snort as much coke as a lot of people." A simple reflection in response would be "You don't snort as much coke as a lot of people." The vocal inflection of the response must turn down at the end, like a statement, rather than turning up at the end like a question. This response allows the client to continue with more social comparison or move to other aspects of cocaine use.

Rephrasing. Rephrasing allows the therapist to test a hypothesis about nuances of meaning in the client's statement based on the context of the conversation. A client may state "I don't snort as much coke as a lot of people," in the midst of a discussion on negative consequences. A rephrasing reflection in response might be "Other folks are worse off than you." Again, the therapist's voice must turn down at the end, like any statement. The rephrased reflection essentially asks a question without asking a question. The reflection "Other folks are worse off than you" asks, in a sense, "Are we talking about how many grams of coke you snort relative to other people you know, or are we actually talking about financial troubles, legal problems, and the fact that your spouse is ready to leave you?" Clients can then elaborate on negative consequences if they are ready, but the therapist is not guiding the interaction to topics the client might not be willing to discuss yet.

Amplified reflection. An amplified reflection takes the client's statement one step further or provides additional emphasis. These reflections often lead clients to clarify the statement or reduce its intensity. When a client says, "I can't imagine a life without drugs," and amplified reflection might be, "You'll probably do them forever." This response might lead the client to reconsider the statement and even

Clinical Pearl (continued)

rephrase it, leading to a comment like, "Well, I don't think people with kids should snort coke." The inflection of these reflections is critical. If the client perceives the reflection as cynical or derisive, the statement will only increase reactance. If the reflection sounds like a simple statement, the client may notice the amplification, disagree with it, and suggest a more moderate version. This suggestion may begin a more elaborate discussion of decreases in use.

Reflecting feeling. As its name suggests, these statements attempt to express the emotion the client may experience. These reflections move the conversation into affect at times when the client seems to be headed in that direction. Few people make dramatic lifestyle changes for reasons that do not involve strong emotions, so exploring feelings has great therapeutic potential. Substance abusing clients may be particularly poor at identifying affect, so tossing out words for emotion can be especially helpful. Even if the therapist does not identify the correct emotion, the reflection gives the client the opportunity to clarify. A reflection of feeling for the statement, "Losing the kids would be a huge drag," might be, "It sounds frustrating." The client may continue with "Actually, it made me really sad." The conversation has moved into an emotional domain with more potential for leading to change. A dry, rational list of reasons may become a more affecting expression of a desire to change.

Double-sided reflection. A double-sided reflection presents both sides of a client's dilemma in a way that communicates empathy but also reveals the discrepancy between some of the client's behaviors and values. These reflections can also help summarize two separate parts of the conversation. Most examples of double-sided reflection use the phrasing, "On one hand X, but on the other hand, Y." A client who previously expressed that a cocaine binge left him too tired to go to work might later emphasize that he does not experience withdrawal. A double-sided reflection might be, "So, on one hand, you don't really have withdrawal but on the other hand, the drug left you too tired to work." The two sides sometimes appear even more discrepant with even blunter wording. A double-sided reflection for a client who wants good grades in school but has missed assignments because of drug use might be, "You want to get a lot of work done and party a lot, too." The presentation of these two contradictory notions can reveal how incongruent a client's desires and actions are, potentially leading to discussions of change.

Agreement with a twist. On occasion, clients make statements that a clinician cannot agree with, but disputing the idea is counterproductive at the time. Part of rolling with the resistance inherent in the change process may require the therapist to acknowledge hearing the point. Agreement with a twist can communicate that the information was received without implying concurrence. A client might say, "If you had my wife, you'd snort a gram once in awhile, too." A reflection that employs agreement with a twist might be, "Some marriages are stressful," or "Wives can have a lot of impact." These allow clients to continue on this topic if they desire or move to other issues. The clinician never has to agree that snorting cocaine is an ideal response to marriage.

Develop Discrepancy

Problem drug users invariably behave in ways that are inconsistent with their other desires, aims, and values. Few, however, face these contradictory actions and ideals in their daily lives. Presenting these incongruent aspects of a client's life in a way that does not resort to confrontation or create reactance is a genuine art. Most forms of reflection can help make these inconsistencies apparent, but amplified and double-sided responses are particularly relevant for developing discrepancy. As the discrepancy becomes more obvious, clients are more likely to consider change, state strong intentions to change, and eventually take action.

Roll with Resistance

Change can be difficult. When a therapist presses a client to change, clients understandably press back. Rather than argue back and forth, the clinician can view resistance as an opportunity to take a different approach. If a client sounds blasé, defiant, or ill-equipped, this need not mean the client is unwilling or unable to change. The client simply may find the discussion uncomfortable. Those clients who have little confidence in their ability to stop using drugs would likely find any prompts to do so quite threatening. Instead of cajoling, pleading, or arguing, the therapist can reflect, reframe, or listen.

Many describe this rolling with resistance using a metaphor related to the martial art of judo. Judo masters rarely counter an opponent's punch by meeting it with another punch, one force directed against another. Instead, they drag the punching arm in the direction the opponent is already moving. In a sense, this makes the opponent's own energy the source of the change. My colleagues who dislike the judo metaphor because of its oppositional implications describe rolling with resistance as a dance. One dance partner can cover for another's misstep by stepping a bit further in the opposite direction, keeping the dance moving without incident. Recognizing reluctance and discussing it as an inherent part of change will often facilitate therapy.

Support Self-Efficacy

Self-efficacy, a term introduced to the field in classic social learning theory work (Bandura, 1977), refers to beliefs about abilities to perform a specific task or behavior. It differs from self-esteem or self-confidence because of its specificity to a given task. Self-esteem or self-confidence often refers to an individual's sense for his or her value or ability in general. Self-efficacy refers to a single skill, like refusing drugs when they are offered or handling negative emotions without drugs. Supporting self-efficacy can transmit positive expectations about a client's skills and abilities, potentially creating a self-fulfilling prophecy of sorts. Nevertheless, it is more than a simple "can do" attitude. A client cannot correctly claim feelings of self-efficacy based on simple cheerleading or demand from the therapist. An adept clinician can build a client's self-efficacy based on genuine assessments of skills and previous behaviors. Clients who have given up one problematic drug might draw on the experience to increase self-efficacy related to giving up another. Those who have performed any difficult, time-consuming, focused task (obtaining a diploma, exercising regularly, finding work) can make comparable claims.

The best buttress for self-efficacy requires building relevant skills. Self-efficacy for refusing drugs when offered will undoubtedly increase more from a role-play about offered drugs than a pep talk. Self-efficacy for handling negative emotions without drugs would likely improve through relaxation training and other strategies. Successive approximations, in which learners master a complex task by first studying its component parts, also can aid self-efficacy. As a client repeatedly engages in the relevant behaviors, self-efficacy should increase, allowing him or her to engage in the behaviors again, subsequently increasing self-efficacy still more. This upward spiral can allow the client to generalize self-efficacy in new ways as well. Developing self-efficacy about refusing drugs may increase optimism about learning to manage negative emotions. Eventually, self-efficacy for eliminating drug problems can increase because self-efficacy for many of the component behaviors has increased.

Readiness to Change

Motivational interviewing combines the general spirit of the treatment with specific techniques to help inspire a shift away from problem drug use. Therapists tailor specific techniques to individual clients, in part by employing them in ways that are consistent with the client's motivation. Guiding self-change requires a view of motivation as a state that can ebb and flow in individuals under different circumstances. The approach consistently stresses that motivation varies naturally with circumstances; it is not an immutable aspect of personality or character. Clients do not come as motivated or unmotivated types. Instead, each person has more or less motivation to change as a result of situational variables, including the social interaction of therapy. Consistent with this idea, motivational interviewing and guided self-change suggest that change is a process that requires different interventions depending upon the client's willingness to act. Tailoring the interventions to clients' levels of motivation keeps sessions focused on the most relevant information for the client at that time. It also may help minimize therapist burnout, since clinicians spend little time on interventions that are irrelevant to the client's need given the current moment. (Discussing relapse prevention with a client who is eager to quit can be remarkably rewarding; the same conversation with someone uninterested in change can prove tense and tedious.)

> Motivational interviewing uses specific techniques to support general strategies

Focusing on readiness is consistent with the popular Stages of Change Model, which describes particular phases that individuals might progress through when altering problem behavior (Prochaska & DiClemente, 2005). By interviewing people who quit smoking cigarettes on their own, researchers suggested six stages common to the process: precontemplation, contemplation, preparation (or determination), action, maintenance, and relapse. Those who rarely or never considered change were said to be in the precontemplation stage. Those debating change were thought to be in the contemplation stage. Those who were planning subsequent new behaviors and buttressing their motivation were said to be in the preparation or determination stage. Those taking steps to apply new behaviors were considered to be in the action stage. Those who had continued action for a while were said to be in the maintenance stage, and those who fell back to old ways were considered in lapse or relapse.

This approach proved popular and provided an interesting short-hand and set of guidelines for intervention. Unfortunately, the measurement of the stages proved problematic (Carey, Purnine, Maistro, & Carey, 1999). The stages did not appear mutually exclusive, and people did not progress through them in the specified order. A continuum of change with multiple contributors may fit both the data and individual experience better (Littrell & Girvin, 2002). Clients may not fit neatly into a distinct stage so much as fluctuate along a continuum of readiness to change. For example, even within session, a client may teeter between what was called contemplation and preparation. Accordingly, a fluid, continuous perspective on motivation and readiness may be the most adaptive approach to take in treatment. Additionally, the stages are also not an immutable quality of the client, but a varying quality of the process of change. Substance abusers are not "contemplators" or even "in the contemplation stage," so much as simply considering their options. Key interventions for different levels of readiness are described below.

A Note on Readiness to Change and Therapist Goals

Clinicians are not immune to maladaptive, automatic, dichotomous thoughts that can deflate even the most enthusiastic and motivated. It's easy to slip into views of clients as "fixed" or "not fixed." An untouted advantage of viewing motivation on a continuum involves the potential to provide more reinforcement for therapists. Client progress is rarely linear, making evaluations difficult. This view of motivation provides fine distinctions along the continuum of change, making progress easier to detect, potentially helping therapists feel good about treatment even if clients are still using drugs. Identifying these changes can help clinicians notice subtle but meaningful alterations in a client's approach to problems, making progress more salient. Any sign of a definite increase in motivation and beginning signs of action should be a cause for enthusiasm. Viewing change as a process benefits the clinician as well as the client. The emphasis on change as a process can help therapists appraise their work in a more self-compassionate way, potentially saving them from dissatisfaction or burnout.

Interventions Tailored to Motivation

Descriptions of readiness to change and the appropriate interventions appear below. As always, the individual techniques may be secondary to the quality of the therapeutic relationship emphasized in previous discussions of the nonspecifics of change. Each technique will work best when presented in the spirit of motivational interviewing, with consistent emphasis on genuineness, nonpossessive warmth, and empathy.

Low Readiness to Change

Many people with problems related to drugs have not considered altering their behavior, and new users typically don't view their consumption as a problem. Nevertheless, even those who haven't given change a thought are still candidates for intervention. An adept therapist would not waste time attempting to teach these people how to quit using; these clients would likely lack motivation to learn these skills. Instead, the therapist would begin with assessment, using approaches like those described in Section 3.

The goal of the assessment would be to raise some doubt about drug use and its connection to negative aspects of a client's life. Those who enter treatment complaining of symptoms that they have not connected to their drug use can benefit dramatically from this approach. A report on the history, amount and frequency of use, as described above, serves as a good start to the assessment process. The therapist would also want to ask about any associated consequences, including negative emotions, fatigue, uncomfortable interpersonal interactions, or any other adverse outcomes. These assessments allow the client to see connections between use and consequences. Those who report labile mood, unpredictable outbursts, insomnia, poor job performance, and a host of other troubles often show surprise that these events coincide with periods of heavy drug consumption. Feedback based on the assessments is ideal for raising doubts about a problem behavior. Providing feedback requires the same nonjudgmental, matter-of-fact approach that motivational interviewing emphasizes. The data from the TLFB and the client's perceptions about norms of drug use can provide a starting point. The TLFB will reveal which drugs the client has used in the previous month. The clinician can then ask for the client's best guess of how many people used this drug in the last month (see Table 2).

Consistent with social psychological theories related to assumed similarity, clients often overestimate how many others use illicit drugs. Fewer than 15% of U.S. citizens have used marijuana in the last month and fewer than 10% have used any other illicit drug. Fewer than 1% of people have used crack cocaine and less than 0.5% have used heroin (see Table 2). Asking clients who qualify for an abuse or dependence diagnosis to guess the rates of these disorders can also be productive. Fewer than 8% of people qualify for an abuse diagnosis and less than 3% qualify for dependence in a lifetime. Substance abusing clients often give estimates two to three times as large as these rates. This feedback about the norms of drug use and problems often can tip the scales in the direction of change, and that incremental increase in readiness is the ideal goal for therapists working with clients who show little initial motivation. A great deal of time may be devoted to reflections and summaries that connect these norms and negative life events to drug use in ways that the client may not have considered. If these connections lead individuals to consider change in any way, they have likely moved toward an ambivalent but detectable level of readiness.

Ambivalent about Change

Ambivalent clients have often considered change more than those who are low in readiness. They may often find themselves weighing the pros and cons of altering actions or continuing the same behavior. If drug use resulted solely in bad experiences, the client would likely have given it up by now. Drugs may have created salient and positive experiences for the client alongside numerous negative consequences. Providing clients with the chance to express this ambivalence may be critical to change. Some therapeutic approaches may view ambivalence as a form of denial. Indeed, an exclusive focus on positive aspects of drug use, especially while ignoring associated problems, certainly seems like denial. Directly confronting the client's ambivalence in an attempt to break through what seems to be denial can potentially harm therapeutic rapport and drive the client away from change. Clients rarely have opportunities to elaborate on any of the positive outcomes they attribute to drug use, at least not in a clinical setting. Permitting a discussion of positive outcomes can go a long way towards building trust and developing a full picture of the contingencies surrounding use. Motivational interviewing focuses on working with, amplifying, and summarizing ambivalence, ultimately in an attempt to reveal the client's own assessment of the costs and benefits of change. One technique that can serve as an ideal springboard for expressing and elaborating on this ambivalence is the decisional balance.

Decisional Balance

The decisional balance, a technique for examining the costs and benefits of change, encourages clients to list pros and cons related to altering problem behaviors (Janis & Mann, 1977). Some research has suggested that the decisional balance alone, particularly in the absence of other aspects of motivational interviewing, may not lead to decreases in drug use. Nevertheless, these studies have not focused on people who were all clearly ambivalent about change at the time. We would not expect individuals who are clearly low or clearly high in readiness to benefit as much from this exercise. Weighing the pros and cons can help clients sort through their ambivalence so they can progress toward higher levels of motivation, particularly when the technique is accompanied by the motivational interviewing style of being with clients (see Figure 5).

The motivational interviewer encourages users to report candidly on all of the benefits of not changing their drug use, all the costs of not changing, all the costs of changing, and all the benefits of changing. Some therapists perform these tasks in a different order, but ending on the benefits of change has the obvious advantage of leaving clients primed to consider the potential rewards of new behavior. The client and therapist then work together to sort through the various factors contributing to the client's feelings about change.

Detailing the benefits of not changing may include a discussion of positive experiences clients have attributed to drug use. These often include any beliefs about relief from boredom, enhanced sexual interactions, enjoyment, slowing of time, making friends, and connections to the counterculture. Then the interviewer asks users to highlight the costs of not changing, emphasizing negative consequences. Reflections on the severity of these consequences can be particularly helpful in this process. The interview then moves to the costs of changing. These costs often echo the benefits of not changing, but clients frequently generate new costs with different emphases that did not appear earlier in the interview. The nonjudgmental, empathic approach on the part of the therapist can allow clients to detail these perceived costs in a way that can reveal if they have unrealistic expectations about the demands and requirements of a new set of actions. This portion of the decisional balance can also

Benefits of NOT Changing	Costs of NOT Changing
• Fun • Stay awake when necessary • More social and talkative	• Trouble with family • Spend too much • Get burned out
Costs of Changing	Benefits of Changing
1. Need new friends 2. Have to get organized 3. Less "rush"	• Save cash • Won't get busted • Less moody

Figure 5
A Sample Decisional Balance from a Stimulant Abuser

be an ideal time to mention novel strategies that have worked for others, giving the client hope that this attempt can be different from previous ones. Next, the interview continues with the benefits of change. Again, these may parallel the costs of not changing, but clients often frame these differently. Reflecting on these benefits and emphasizing their long-term impact can help clients resolve some of their ambivalence about change.

Additional questions can serve as a nice way to summarize the decisional balance exercise, encourage further elaboration, and wrap up. Three ideal questions are:

1) What would it take to increase the costs of not changing?
2) What would it take to increase the benefits of change?
3) Where do you see this behavior going in the near future?

Clients often reveal that the costs of not changing seem relatively minor in the present, but when prompted about the trajectory they are on, they realize that their current behavior cannot continue indefinitely. A perspective on the future may increase the benefits of change. Clients also appreciate the opportunity to elaborate on their hopes and dreams for what the benefits will be.

A skilled clinician can gather a great deal of data on a client's beliefs about drug use from this exercise, including some expectancies about drugs that may be worthy of challenge later in therapy. The stimulant abuser who claims "It's the only way I can get through my day!" or the sedative abuser who emphasizes, "There's no other way to sleep," reveals cognitions that will be important to dispute. This exercise can also reveal if a client's expectations about change are realistic. Some clients who have used drugs for many years and experienced dramatic negative consequences somehow think that bells will ring and birds will sing once they stop. Although difficulties with labile mood, fatigue, fear of legal repercussions, and the negative impact of intoxication are bound to improve, other problems will remain. The clinician can emphasize that these problems will also likely benefit from therapy. In addition, they will be easier to handle once the complications related to drug use decrease. New problems can appear to emerge at this time in surprising ways, including some that may have motivated problematic drug use in the first place. Clients with less than optimal skills at social interaction, mood management, self-regulation, and organization may find these troubles more obvious when frequent intoxication is no longer part of their lives. Assuring them that therapy can also assist with these issues may make behavior change sound less daunting.

Initial assessments of pros and cons often reveal strong desires to continue using as well as equally strong desires to stop. This situation may reflect the ambivalence people feel about altering their consumption of drugs. The objective of this exercise is, in fact, to explore the ambivalent, conflicted nature of these decisions to use. There's no need to rush this process. Ambivalence serves as a common and important component of increasing motivation. During further discussion, the therapist respectfully reflects the users' concerns back to them, emphasizing the negative consequences that they generated earlier. These reflections often uncover new negative consequences that the client had not connected to drug use. This process often leads problem users to a decision to change. A firm decision to change is an obvious sign of increased motivation.

Envisioning

A frequent phenomenon that has received little attention is envisioning – those client comments that reveal some projection into a future without problematic drug use. Statements like "Who would my friends be if I didn't smoke pot?" or "How would I get through the day without speed to pick me up?" reflect envisioning. At first blush these comments may sound like resistance. The clients appear to be offering a reason for not changing. Nevertheless, these statements suggest that the clients are contemplating a future with different behaviors. They are not denying a willingness to change so much as expressing concerns about what would happen if they do. Simple reflections can certainly help in response to client envisioning, but questions that encourage the client to generate options for solving predicted problems may make the future changes seem more appealing.

Thus, "Who would my friends be if I didn't smoke pot?" might be met with, "Who are your friends who don't smoke pot now?" or "Have you ever had friends who didn't smoke pot?" or even "Do you think your friends would force you to smoke pot if you didn't want to?" Queries like "How would I get through the day without speed?" might lead to responses like "Was there a time when you went without stimulants?" or "Do you know anyone who makes it through a busy day without speed?" or even "How did you get through days before?" Encouraging clients to go on with their envisioning and plan for the problems they foresee can help them make the transition to increased readiness for change.

Increased Readiness

Clients with increased readiness to change often begin with a clearly stated desire to alter actions. This level of readiness serves as the appropriate time for a drug user and a clinician to formulate a plan for changing consumption. This is an ideal opportunity to increase resolve, fortitude, and general grit for the process. Note that any attempts to devise a strategy for change before the client has this much motivation would essentially waste effort. Motivation must increase before a plan can succeed. This time can be an enjoyable one for clinicians as they watch how a realistic plan can increase motivation, which in turn encourages continued and detailed planning of a change strategy, which in turn enhances motivation again.

Change Strategy

Designing and examining the barriers to a strategy for changing drug use is essential. The plan often stems from brainstorming between the interviewer and the client. Any promising options for the plan deserve consideration, particularly those generated by the client. Clients are more likely to adhere to a plan of their own construction. The key to evaluations of plans relies a lot on the spirit of motivational interviewing, particularly genuineness. Clinicians can ask if previous attempts at changing use employed the proposed strategy, how they turned out, and what the client thinks will make this attempt work. In addition, explaining apprehensions about the plan need not seem like raining on a client's parade. Clients need feedback if their plans sound too unrealistic, difficult, or unworkable.

The drug user may now desire to participate in a 12-step program or other group support system. Referrals that include details about meeting times, locations, and directions as well as an introduction to 12-step volunteers lead to better outcomes under these circumstances (Timko & DeBenedetti, 2007). The plan might include providing training in new ways to handle negative emotions and difficult situations. The strategy for change may rely on techniques from cognitive-behavioral therapy, like avoiding classically conditioned stimuli that might lead to craving, planning to fill time with behaviors incompatible with drug use, and altering maladaptive beliefs, as detailed below.

Avoiding Classically Conditioned Stimuli

The repeated pairing of various cues with drug use and intoxication leads to strong classically conditioned responses. The presence of drug cues can increase several subjective reactions, including craving, withdrawal, anxiety, and tension. Physiological changes also accompany exposure to drug cues, including changes in skin conductance, skin temperature, salivation, heart rate, and blood flow in the brain. All of these subjective and physiological reactions seem to contribute to relapse. Drug users who show the greatest reactivity to cues are also the most likely to return to drug use. Like any classically conditioned response, these reactions to drug cues should extinguish if they are presented repeatedly in the absence of drugs, the unconditioned stimulus.

Researchers have been remarkably innovative in the creation of ideographic sets of drug cues tailored to individual users, even applying virtual reality technology on occasion, but this hard work has rarely translated to documented improvements in treatment outcome. Comparable cue-exposure approaches have helped clients with obsessive compulsive disorder and anxiety disorder. Some reactivity to cues dissipates for alcoholics exposed to their favorite beverages, smokers exposed to cigarettes and a lighter, and opiate addicts exposed to drug paraphernalia. Despite the intuitive appeal of these approaches, outcome studies on cue exposure treatments remain relatively rare. In addition, results have not been as impressive as one might hope. Cue exposure may decrease some measures of alcohol involvement in alcoholics, but abstinence rates do not seem to improve significantly at follow-up (see Marissen, Franken, Blanken, an den Brink, & Hendriks, 2005, for a review). Contrary to expectations, one randomized control trial found that opiate addicts in cue-exposure treatment were more likely to drop out and more likely to relapse (Marissen et al., 2007).

These results suggest that exposure to cues may prove too individualized and tricky to lend itself to homogeneous group interventions. In the initial stages of treatment, avoiding classically conditioned stimuli that might increase craving may be the most adaptive approach. Many of the most obvious cues appear in the functional analysis of drug use. Twelve-step work devoted to identifying persons, places, and things associated with drug use is comparably useful. Those cues that cannot be avoided (e.g., Friday night), serve as potential high-risk situations. These situations require concrete, detailed plans for coping.

Alternative Activities

Increasing activities, particularly those that are incompatible with drug use, can help minimize lapses as well as improve mood. Clients can generate a list of actions that can fill their time and help them achieve other goals. Activities can prove particularly helpful when handling craving, sadness, and boredom. A list of reliable distracting behaviors can help clients prepare for high risk situations. These activities generally fall into domains related to relationships, personal growth, health, social action, career, and entertainment. Visiting non-using friends, writing in a journal, exercising, volunteering, taking a class, and reading can all provide enjoyment without requiring extensive preparation, time, or resources.

Planning a week's worth of pleasant activities can reveal if client expectations are realistically balanced in a number of ways. If their daily activities are consistent with bigger goals, and their plans ensure enough fun, they are more likely to stick to plans and reap the benefits. Initial lists can be extensive but often lack the sort of regular tasks that appear in most average days. Few of us can visit a museum, go hunting, and ride a hot air balloon every day. Again, balance is crucial. Five consecutive days of "Get dressed, eat, go to work, come home, exercise, clean the house, go to bed" can be an invitation to a weekend of relapse. The key is to combine frequent fun with tasks that build a sense of accomplishment to lay a foundation for long-term progress.

Altering Beliefs

Challenging maladaptive beliefs can improve many symptoms

Drug-related beliefs that suggest cognitive distortions often reveal themselves at this point in treatment, giving the clinician the opportunity to train clients to challenge ideas that are incorrect or maladaptive. Working on other maladaptive beliefs about the self, the world, and the future can prove useful as well. Typical drug-related beliefs include thoughts like, "I can't get through the day without some sort of pick-me-up," "The only way to end craving is to use," and "Drugs are the only way to make life fun." Clients often have superb intuitions about which thoughts are more likely to increase the risk of drug use. Clinicians can prepare clients for altering maladaptive beliefs by emphasizing a few key points. Thoughts like these can appear at any time but are no indication of a lack of progress. These thoughts are easier to handle once clients have learned to recognize them, and they will continue to occur months or years after quitting. Once clients can separate which thoughts are more conducive to lapses, accept that thoughts like these will appear unpredictably, and emphasize that these are simply thoughts, not a demand for any specific behavior, they can confront these maladaptive ideas in a number of ways. Generally, challenging the thoughts and focusing on alternative thoughts about the benefits of new behavior and negative consequences of use can be helpful.

Challenging

Once clients identify a thought or belief that they suspect is less than ideal, they can challenge the belief through questions. Helpful questions can include: Is there any evidence that this thought is really true, all the time? On a scale from 0 (not at all) to 10 (absolutely): How much do I really believe this thought? If someone else told me this, would I believe it? Is there a better way to think about this? Other techniques that can prove helpful for altering maladaptive thoughts related to drug use, negative mood, or ill-advised actions include recalling benefits of not using as well as the negative consequences of use.

Clinical Pearl
Challenging Beliefs

Identified belief: Drugs are the only way to make life fun.

Query 1: Is there any evidence that this thought is really true, all the time?

Client response: Well, it's partly true, sort of, but not really true. I've had a lot of fun with drugs. There are other ways to have fun; that's true. Drugs are actually only fun for a little while and then they turn into a hassle one way or another.

Query 2: On a scale from 0 (not at all) to 10 (absolutely) how much do I really believe this thought?

Client response: Actually, I don't think that drugs are the ONLY way to make life fun, even though I've acted that way some times. I guess I'd say about a 4.

Query 3: If someone else told me this, would I believe it?

Client response: Not really. I see tons of people having fun every day and I doubt that they're all on drugs.

Query 4: Is there a better way to think about this?

Client response: Probably. I'm not going to deny that I've had some fun times on drugs, but I also paid the price. I'd probably do better to think that there are lots of ways to have fun and drugs don't end up being much fun in the long run.

Comment. Note that repeating this process may not make this thought disappear so much as weaken its believability. Soon clients learn to recognize thoughts like these as merely thoughts and not as indisputable facts. The idea that drugs are the only way to make life fun may occur to this client again, but it will seem less credible and less likely to lead to a lapse.

Altering Beliefs by Listing or Recalling Benefits of Not Using

A list of the benefits of not using can help clients in a number of ways. Some of the benefits generated for the decisional balance exercise can serve as a start for a brief but pointed list of the most positive effects of new behaviors. Ideally, clients could carry this list, or some representation of its items (e.g., a picture of their family), with them wherever they go. This list or the representative items can serve as a reminder of the benefits of the changes they have made. Priming these benefits can also alter the believability of certain thoughts. Thoughts like "Drugs are the only way to make life fun" seem less true after reviewing benefits of reduced use like improved health, self-esteem, relationships, mood, and work. Some clients also view the content of the thought in different ways once they have reviewed the benefits of their new behavior. One client put it nicely when examining the thought "Drugs are the only way to make life fun." In light of his list of benefits, he said, "I don't need that kind of fun bad enough to ditch all these other things."

A list of the benefits of not using might include: I feel better about myself, I have more cash, I'm doing a great job at work, My ex-wife and I fight less, I enjoy my time with my kids more, I'm less moody, my sleep is better, and I feel healthier.

Altering Beliefs by Reviewing or Recalling Negative Consequences

An alternative to reviewing the benefits of not using involves reviewing the negative consequences of use. Many maladaptive thoughts about drug use involve positive expectations of outcomes. Those who believe that drug use creates good experiences are often the most likely to lapse (see Marlatt, 2002). Most positive expectancies about drug use prove hard to dispute because they are essentially true in the short run. Thoughts like "Cocaine will make me happy," may fit a great deal of a client's learning history. Expectations about negative consequences are often more difficult to prime, perhaps because they involve outcomes that occur later than the positive effects. Thoughts like "Cocaine will make me tired and irritable," may be as true as the positive expectancies, but the outcome is less immediate than the acute euphoria that might arise soon after snorting the drug.

In an effort to make these negative consequences more salient, clients can review a previously written list or generate a new list when difficult situations or maladaptive thoughts arise. Negative consequences related to physical and mental health, social skills, family functioning, school and work, peer relationships, and leisure can all work as good reminders of how drug use has gone awry in the past. Generating an extensive catalog of bad outcomes and picking the most salient or aversive to form a pocket-sized list can be an ideal approach. A sample client's negative consequences might include: all the lies I told, all those fights with girlfriends, the time I hit the mailbox with the car, that embarrassing meeting at work where I flew off the handle, that stupid bar fight, the time I cussed David out, the money I blew when the kids needed shoes, how I felt having to borrow money from Mom, all those missed Mondays at work that made me have to stay late the rest of the week.

Generalizing Challenges to Maladaptive Cognitions

Substance abuse is highly comorbid with other disorders that respond well to cognitive-behavioral interventions, particularly anxiety and depression. Techniques for disputing maladaptive thoughts related to drug use work comparably well for challenging cognitions associated with anxiety, depression, and other disorders. Clients who have learned to recognize beliefs that are conducive to drug use can be quick to identify thoughts that can precede other maladaptive behaviors. The queries that can challenge maladaptive drug-related thoughts can also help challenge beliefs that can heighten anxiety, negative mood, or ill-advised action.

Implementing Change

Once clients regularly alter old behaviors in favor of new ones, they are essentially taking real steps rather than debating about readiness. They no longer merely consider change; they actually *do* change. The genuine experience of new behaviors and actions can reveal valuable information unanticipated when they planned these new events. Some aspects of reduction or controlled use may prove unexpectedly difficult. In contrast, clients may find some situations easier than they expected. The motivational interviewers must now help adapt the strategies constructed earlier in treatment to the realities of active change, offering more effective methods in difficult areas and limiting ineffective or unnecessary strategies. The interviewer also offers reassurance that the process will become less difficult over time and the new behaviors will grow easier with practice. They will help clients solve emerging problems and unanticipated situations related to use. They will listen attentively to detailed descriptions of difficulties and proud retellings of resisted temptations. This is also a key time for increasing a public commitment to new behaviors. An abundance of literature from social psychology documents that telling other people about one's own behavior change can help maintain the changes. Clients can choose to discuss their new behaviors with other individuals in their social circles, potentially adding social support while simultaneously increasing public commitment.

The beginning of new behaviors can be a particularly important time for praise. The natural reinforcers for new behaviors will certainly be rewarding, but extra congratulations from the therapist can be critical. Clients may have few people in their social circles who can genuinely commend them on eliminating drug problems. Many of their friends may not have known about their troubles. Those that do may not be comfortable mentioning it. Consistent and specific acknowledgments of progress can mean a great deal to clients. These moments of praise may require that therapists attend to their own emotions in order to stay genuine in the interaction while still providing as much enthusiasm for progress as possible. Although client and therapist may have both seen comparable changes before, the novel aspects of current changes deserve emphasis. Reminders that this progress and the associated effort is a happy event can be frequent and effusive, even if the new behaviors no longer seem particularly challenging.

Maintenance

After a steady period of new behaviors, clients may report increased confidence in their skills. This new sense of self-efficacy suggests that preparing to maintain changes would be productive. Self-efficacy and sustained change are the keys to maintenance. This is the ideal time to reinforce the commitment to new behaviors. Cheering for clients as they progress, reminding them of how far they have come, and summarizing all the changes that they have made can help them view the new behaviors in the most positive light. Client and therapist will work together now to prevent relapse. They will identify alternative positive behaviors so clients can use time more adaptively while maintaining a balance of productivity and fun. They will identify situations that put the user at high risk for relapse and plan ways to avoid problematic use in these circumstances. For example, clients may decide to avoid parties where drugs are present. They may role-play refusing drugs if they are offered. They may practice relaxation techniques if tension often preceded their drug use. They may call a hot line or a friend in times of temptation. Note that these techniques for preventing relapse are consistent with 12-step and cognitive-behavioral approaches. This overlap might contribute to the comparable results of these different programs.

Lapse and Relapse

Occasional backsliding occurs in many efforts to alter behavior. Original studies of people who quit smoking cigarettes reveal that they rarely remain abstinent on their first try (Prochaska & DiClemente, 2005). They quit, lapse, relapse, and quit again. Proponents of motivational interviewing and guided self-change consider lapses and relapses as another aspect of readiness. From this perspective, the occasional slip is a common, and even an expected, occurrence. The inclusion of lapses as part of the process sets these strategies apart from many other approaches to altering drug problems. Instead of seeing use of a small amount of a drug (e.g., a puff of a marijuana joint) as grounds to restart the entire program, the event is considered a lapse, another potential consequence of the difficulty inherent in altering an established behavior.

Mentioning that lapses happen need not turn into a self-fulfilling prophecy. Considering lapses as a part of the change process also decreases the chances of transforming a slip into a full-blown relapse, the *abstinence violation effect*. The abstinence violation effect occurs when former users consume a small amount of a drug, view this small lapse as a catastrophe of some sort, and subsequently go on to use large amounts or for extended periods because they "blew it." Emphasizing that a lapse did not turn into a binge can increase a sense of self-efficacy and diminish demoralization. The key to lapses parallels the key to maintenance: preventing relapse. Lapses require immediate action. Lapsing drug users can prevent relapse by rapidly exiting the situation and removing the chance of continued use.

Many who lapse berate themselves, and clinicians working with clients at these moments can take important steps to avoid the demoralization that could transform the lapse into a relapse. A productive use of their time and energy requires identifying the precursors to the drug use. Simple questions about what happened immediately prior to the drug use, and immediately prior to that, can prove illustrative. A frank examination may reveal a new high-risk situation, providing the opportunity to formulate a plan for how to handle this predicament in the future. These steps should work in the same way that previous functional analyses worked. For example, a former cannabis smoker may find himself lighting up after a fight with a family member. This situation may not be one that he had identified as high risk before. Now he knows that he needs to plan new ways to deal with conflict. He can turn this lapse into a learning experience to prevent later use. Thus, lapses remain a part of the change process; planning for them may minimize problems. By combining good therapeutic skills in general and targeted interventions for each level of readiness, a motivational interviewer can help problem drug users through many steps toward minimizing troubles.

Guided self-change uses motivational interviewing techniques to keep clients encouraged about change, making the most common problem in conducting treatment the prevention of relapse. Relapse prevention, an overarching term for a set of strategies designed to eliminate a return to problematic drug use, relies on identifying potential triggers and high-risk situations in an effort to minimize their impact on clients. The details of the relapse prevention model can grow extensive; one review presents the relapse process with over 20 boxes and 25 arrows. A simpler approach suggests that key conditions make maintaining abstinence easier. Taking steps to ensure these conditions can help guarantee fewer problems.

Relapse Defined

Identifying key conditions requires a definition of relapse. The meaning of relapse varies but becomes more precise when considered relative to lapse and prolapse. A lapse is an initial return to the problem behavior, a slip-up in the maintenance of change. A client who finds an old prescription stimulant hidden in a drawer, takes it, realizes it's against his best interest, and throws the remaining pills down the drain, has experienced a lapse. A relapse would be a more elaborate return to the problem behavior, one that included a longer duration than a mere lapse, more like "falling off the wagon." A client who finds an old prescription stimulant hidden in a drawer, takes it, buys more, and continues to take them for a month, has clearly relapsed.

A prolapse is a return to the change process, essentially "getting back on the horse" and returning to abstinence or previously established goals of use. Ideally, clients would experience no lapses, making relapses impossible and prolapses unnecessary. But lapses are common. As an alternative, relapse prevention identifies predictors of lapses in an effort to minimize their occurrence. Nevertheless, given the frequency of lapses and their inherent role in change, additional relapse prevention techniques focus on eliminating the transition from lapse to relapse. This approach relies on the identification of specific, personalized high-risk situations. Although entire books are devoted to relapse prevention, a few central strategies can account for a great deal of improvement. Two ideas play an important role in relapse prevention generally as well as the assessment of high-risk situations: the abstinence violation effect and apparently irrelevant decisions.

Abstinence Violation

As mentioned, the abstinence violation effect occurs when clients slip, use a small amount of a drug or exceed their stated limit, and decide that since they have already made the small mistake they might as well use more. For example, a client inattentively takes a puff from an offered joint, realizes his mistake, but continues to smoke for the rest of the night. Those of us who splurge a bit by overeating at a nice dinner out only to return home and eat everything in the refrigerator have a similar experience. Note how abstinence violation appears to rest on a maladaptive cognition: once I use any amount of the drug, I have failed, therefore I might as well use excessively. Once the outcome of a situation is defined dichotomously as success or failure, there is no room for gradations of either outcome (Beck et al., 2005). Dichotomous thinking like this is common in a number of disorders and lends itself well to intervention (particularly cognitive-behavioral intervention). Targeting maladaptive cognitions cannot only help with relapse prevention, but can also improve related psychological problems. Much of relapse prevention focuses on avoiding the abstinence violation effect. The assessment of high-risk situations invariably lays the groundwork for extensive preparation for handling these moments.

Apparently Irrelevant Decisions

Apparently irrelevant decisions are small, seemingly minor thoughts and actions that actually increase the probability of a lapse (Marlatt, 2002). Some examples seem obvious in retrospect, but they often do not seem apparent during treatment. A client struggling with prescription opiates who keeps a full bottle of hydrocodone in the cabinet in case of injury has made a decision that will contribute to risk for lapses. The former marijuana smoker who attends the local hemp festival to show support for friends is walking into a high-risk situation. The reformed cocaine user who drives past the location of known dealers in an effort to check out the old neighborhood has essentially increased the availability of the drug. Each choice might seem inconsequential at the time, but the sum of a few of them can create predicaments that tax the coping skills of anyone trying to minimize drug problems. A slight move in a potentially difficult direction can appear trivial at first but turn into a tough set of circumstances a few hours later.

Clients who fail to grasp the idea of apparently irrelevant decisions often respond well to the idea of the *trim tab,* a metaphor attributed to Buckminster Fuller. A trim tab is essentially a miniature rudder connected to the bottom of a big rudder, which connects to a large boat. Moving a large boat in the water is very difficult, which is why these boats have a rudder. The rudder is easier to move in a specific direction, and once the rudder has turned, the boat turns in the same direction. On particularly large boats, the rudder is also correspondingly large, making it difficult to turn. These large rudders have a trim tab beneath, which functions as a small rudder for the large rudder. The trim tab is easier to turn. Once the trim tab turns in the desired direction, the rudder turns more easily, and then the boat turns more easily. A minor change in direction early in a voyage can mean dramatically different destinations later. Each move of the trim tab sends the rudder in a certain direction, and the boat as well. Each little decision can bump a client slightly in a certain direction, but that slight bump can mean dramatically different outcomes later.

With this metaphor in mind, some of the insidious aspects of apparently irrelevant decisions become clear. Even the most innocuous choices can increase the chance of a lapse. Imagine this series of decisions. A former crack cocaine user could pick up his payroll check or have it deposited directly in the bank. The decision seems inconsequential, and direct deposit might require filling out complex, time-consuming forms. Picking up the check personally requires taking it to the bank. Taking the check to the bank requires another decision. Cash it now or make a deposit? The decision to cash the check also seems minor at the time. A trip to the grocery store may seem a good idea. If memory serves, the store in the old neighborhood has a locally made brand of soda that is a personal favorite. Buying something special to enjoy seems like a good reward for the latest progress. The trip would also support local business, so it sounds like a good idea. Suddenly "out of the blue," the client is near a crack house with a pocket full of cash. Note how three small decisions (picking up a check rather than having it deposited directly, cashing the check rather than depositing it, and driving to a different store) create a difficult situation even though no single decision appears particularly problematic. Clients often respond well to stories of apparently irrelevant decisions and may enjoy telling a story of relapse that includes some of their own. These serve as ideal opportunities for identifying high-risk situations.

High-Risk Situations

Identifying high risk situations can help prevent relapse

Research on relapse prevention began with the study of participants in drug treatment programs who had lapsed. A thorough assessment of the situations and events that preceded the lapse helped provide valuable information for fashioning the relapse prevention program. Initial work suggested that lapses were particularly likely to occur immediately following a large set of identifiable events. The events generally fell into interpersonal and intrapersonal categories.

1) Interpersonal High-Risk Situations. Interpersonal events, as the name implies, involve interactions with others. Some of these interactions involve general conflict. Other interactions specifically concern drugs. In the research on high-risk situations, many clients who lapsed reported that a frustrating interaction with another person precipitated their use. A fight with a parent, partner, or friend often occurred immediately prior to lapses. Clients who report heavy previous use or lapses after these sorts of interpersonal interactions often benefit from social skills training, particularly those sessions that emphasize assertiveness. Those who learn to make assertive requests, reject unjust or inaccurate criticism, and express negative emotions in productive ways can handle interpersonal conflict without returning to problematic use of substances.

Other participants in the research who lapsed emphasized another sort of social interaction that occurred prior to use; people around them had provided incentives or pressure to return to use. Social pressure is often direct. When others offer drugs directly, express disappointment about other people's abstinence, or criticize clients for not using, the pressure is obvious and easy to identify. Other social pressure is more indirect but equally troublesome. Others may seek out the client to express enthusiasm about the quality of a new batch of drugs, elaborate on delightful intoxication experiences, or denigrate acquaintances who have stopped using. Though these others have not actually offered drugs to the client, the social subtext is clear. Clients who report events like these often benefit from careful planning about social interactions as well as practiced drug refusal skills.

2) Intrapersonal High Risk Situations. In addition to these social interactions, many who lapsed reported intrapersonal experience that preceded their use. These generally fell into categories related to extremes in emotion or reactions to drugs and their cues. Both joy and sorrow preceded lapses in many cases. Negative affect commonly leads to drug use, particularly among those who believe that drugs can put an end to these feelings. Most drug users have temporarily alleviated bad moods with drugs repeatedly. Surprisingly, a good mood can also precede lapses, especially among those who think that drugs can enhance positive emotion. Those trained in alternative ways to manage mood have a better chance of maintaining progress in these circumstances.

Physical states related to drugs also precede lapses frequently. A common physical state that increases the risk of a lapse is withdrawal. The negative affect and physical discomfort associated with the absence of the drug disappears rapidly when clients use again, making this a particularly tough time. Identifying withdrawal can actually prove surprisingly tricky. Drugs taken in high doses over long periods may not clear from the body rapidly. The first day of abstinence after a long period of opiate or stimulant use can be deceptively easy. Clients may not realize that sadness and aches days after quitting might arise from withdrawal, leading them to misattribute these woes to something else. Normalizing these symptoms, taking extra care to eat appropriately, get plenty of rest and fluids, and minimizing stress can make withdrawal tolerable.

Another set of drug-related physical states concerns craving, urges, and temptations to use. An intense subjective desire to use often precedes lapses. These often occur in the presence of cues for the drug. Classically conditioned responses to almost anything previously paired repeatedly with drugs can lead to powerful longing for the drug itself. Obvious correlates of drug use, including finding hidden drugs, coming across paraphernalia, or walking near old locations, often lead to craving. Less obvious cues can also have large effects. A specific time of day (the notorious 4:20 associated with marijuana lore) or days of the week (payday, the weekend) can elicit urges. Works of art related to drugs, including movies that depict use or songs about addiction, could serve as remarkable precursors to lapses. Sometimes the presence of a cue elicits little reaction. Under ideal circumstances, paraphernalia or even the drug itself might fail to elicit urges of any kind. Nevertheless, the same cue might lead to tremendous craving when the client is in a deflated, fatigued, or emotional state.

Exposure to these cues can undo some of the classically conditioned reactions, but this process can be difficult and is certainly not a linear, stepwise decrease in reactivity. Each time a client confronts a cue without using, the strength of the classically conditioned reactions should decrease. Some inpatient programs have employed cue exposure techniques, including leading clients through all of the steps of drug administration in the absence of the drug. The exposure to cues appears to decrease arousal and improve outcomes in some work (Sitharthan, Sitharthan, Hough, & Kavanagh, 1997). Other studies find that cue exposure increases drop out and relapse (Marissen et al., 2007).

Other cravings and urges appear to arise even in the absence of any cues. Sometimes the cues may have appeared outside the individual's awareness. Alternatively, a craving may arise unexpectedly. These situations are difficult to prevent but reinforce the idea that handling craving is essential to relapse prevention. Other physical states that can precede drug use include any alteration in biological functioning. Many clients who have used drugs extensively have paired them with physical illness, fatigue, hunger, and arousal.

Research on different predictors of lapses laid the foundation for identifying triggers and high-risk situations that is essential for understanding the relapse process (Marlatt, 2002). A familiarity with the general categories of high-risk situations will facilitate assessment of those that are most important to an individual client. An ideal way to identify seemingly irrelevant decisions and associated high-risk situations is the functional analysis, a detailed assessment of the precursors, correlates, and consequences of drug use.

Identifying High-Risk Situations: The Functional Analysis

The general categories of high-risk situations include interpersonal events like conflict as well as direct and indirect social pressures. Intrapersonal events include extremes in emotion (both positive and negative), and physical states like withdrawal. Temptations and urges also can be risky situations. These include moments when cues are present as well as many when no obvious cues appear. Other physical states, particularly pain, hunger, fatigue, and general discomfort are common high-risk situations. In addition, users occasionally test their personal control by purposely exposing themselves to cues. These broad categories are helpful but clinicians can identify specific high-risk situations for each user with the functional analysis.

A functional analysis of drug use answers several questions about the predictors, correlates, and consequences. This information will help identify high-risk situations. The client's latest use of drugs, a recent session of extensive use, or an example with particularly negative consequences can serve as a good beginning for a functional analysis. Assess what drugs were used and in what amounts. What happened at the time of use? Who was present? What was the location? What was the client doing at the time? What was the client thinking? How was the client feeling? This information is central to understanding use itself.

A couple of caveats about assessments of thoughts and feelings may prove helpful. Reporting thoughts can be difficult. Clients often say that they were not thinking anything at the time they were using. Others report self-evident or obvious cognitions (e.g., "I thought, 'I sure would like to smoke some pot!'"). Repeated queries, however, often reveal specific expectations about stressors, drug effects, social skills, and other factors that will prove useful in relapse prevention (e.g., "These pills will calm me down and I won't blab too much at the party."). A thorough assessment of these thoughts also lays the groundwork for discussions of the link between cognitions, affect, and risk for relapse.

Substance users show elevated rates of *alexithymia,* a diminished capacity to identify or express their own emotions. Alexithymic clients may respond better to interventions that are more strictly cognitive and behavioral than those that focus on enhancing motivation through more affective means (Rosenblum et al., 2005). The assessment of feelings with these clients has its quirks. Many begin with no vocabulary for emotion at all, and list physical sensations when asked about feelings (e.g., "I felt sick," or "it gave me a headache"). Others progress to reporting two terms that they view as feelings: "good" and "bad." Providing a list of options can help (sad, mad, glad, afraid, disgusted, etc.). Some respond to queries about how they think other people would feel in the same situation. Coaching clients to improve their skill at identifying their emotions has the potential to decrease relapse. The client who is unable to distinguish between negative affect and drug cravings or urges is more likely to choose an ineffective coping strategy in the presence of what seems to them to be amorphous arousal. Learning to identify specific feelings can help clients choose appropriate ways to accept, modulate, or enjoy their emotional experiences.

After identifying relevant thoughts and feelings, assess the consequences. What happened at the end of the session of use and afterward? What did the client think? How did the client feel? After the consequences, assess what happened immediately prior to use. The same questions used for assessing the circumstances of use apply. An ideal way to uncover apparently irrelevant decisions essentially repeats the question "What happened immediately before that?"

The following example will help illustrate how the functional analysis works and how it can uncover seemingly irrelevant decisions, high-risk situations, drug expectancies, and foci for treatment.

Clinical Pearl
Functional Analysis

Drug used and amount: 40 mg of Ritalin (snorted), 4 glasses of wine, 2 Ambien

Who was present? Me

What were you doing? Grinding pills and cutting them into lines. I was going to write a paper but ended up playing video games, cleaning the stove, and watching part of a movie.

What were you thinking? First I thought that this would be a great way to get all of this work done. Then when I couldn't actually write I thought about how I've snorted Ritalin before thinking I would get stuff done and it never really works. Then I thought I might as well clean the apartment since I can't work. After the first two pills, I thought I might as well enjoy myself and do two more. Those two made me too edgy, so I opened a bottle of wine. Then I thought I needed the Ambien to crash.

How were you feeling? Excited at first. Then I got frustrated with the paper because I was too amped up. I got mad at myself and felt bad about school. Then I got worried that I wouldn't be able to sleep.

Consequences: Didn't get the paper done. Didn't really have fun because I had the paper in the back of my mind the whole time. Didn't really clean up well because I was just bouncing around. The top of the stove was perfect and the rest was still a mess. Couldn't watch the whole movie because I was too wound up. Missed class the next morning because I was so tired and ended up having to eat some more pills to make it through the day at work. Had to email the teaching assistant and beg for an extension on the paper since I didn't get it done.

What were you thinking? That I was an idiot to think that this drug was somehow going to help me get work done. That I must have more of a problem with this than I keep pretending that I do, or I wouldn't find myself in this same situation over and over.

How were you feeling? Sad. Angry at myself.

What happened before use?: I had put the paper off all weekend. I sat for about half an hour looking at the screen and couldn't get rolling. I was feeling kind of groggy and hung over.

What were you thinking? That the Ritalin would help me get the words on the page.

How were you feeling? Anxious about getting the paper done. Hopeful that the pages would start churning out once I got going.

What happened before that?: I went out the night before with Julie and Bill and got high, ate a Vicodin, and drank too much.

What were you thinking? That I should have done the paper during the day but I couldn't back out on those two because I keep canceling on them. I could have only had a couple drinks but once I got high that night I sort of let loose.

How were you feeling? I felt a whole bunch of different things. I'm sort of bored with Julie and Bill and a little angry at them for giving me trouble about not hanging out with them more. I was worried about the paper and mad at myself for putting it off.

Apparently irrelevant decisions?: Putting off the paper. Scheduling time with friends when work isn't scheduled or isn't complete. Partying when I've got work to do the next day.

High risk situation?: When work isn't planned ahead.

Clinical Pearl (continued)

Comment. Note how the in-depth functional analysis of this single event revealed multiple targets for intervention. The client uncovered potential problems with time management, study skills, drug expectancies, social skills, assertiveness, and abstinence violation. Identifying the apparently irrelevant decision to procrastinate on the paper essentially establishes this minor situation as one that is high risk for relapse. That is, procrastinating on an assignment should be considered potentially hazardous for drug abuse. If the client can accept poor planning of an assignment as an example of a high-risk situation, the opportunity for training in problem solving also arises. The client could benefit from keeping a date book and planning adequate time to complete assignments ahead of deadlines. Training in these relatively simple skills could be essential. A therapist can challenge resistance to the idea of this type of planning by using a decisional balance and other motivational interviewing techniques, essentially making the time management a new target behavior. Homework assignments that emphasize planning ahead for assignments could prove particularly helpful here. Few clients will regret finishing a project before it is due.

The assessment also reveals a maladaptive expectancy about drug use in this setting: an intranasal stimulant will help writing. Problem drug users frequently expect drugs to enhance performance, even in the absence of evidence. Even in clients with attention deficit problems, an insufflated stimulant will likely lead to too much arousal to allow for appropriate focus and concentration for writing. The client mentions thinking that this strategy had failed in the past. Delineating the accuracy of this belief can be a productive path for challenging the expectation. In addition, even if the belief were true, it obviously has maladaptive consequences. If a stimulant improved writing in some way, the negative consequences likely outweigh any advantages. As a harm reduction technique, alternative stimulants, particularly the ubiquitous caffeine, might make a better option for staying awake to finish an assignment. The client may agree that smaller blocks of writing time under less pressure from the deadline would probably create better results.

Aspects of the client's social skills also unfold from this assessment. The client mentions ambivalence about spending time with two acquaintances who apparently use drugs. An assertive decline of their offer to spend time together, even despite their cajoling about how infrequently they see him, could have prevented at least one and perhaps two incidents of problematic drug consumption. This information can spearhead a conversation about the number of friends the client has who do not use drugs. It can also lead to an examination of social skills and support.

Finally, the functional analysis reveals some dichotomous thinking related to increasing dosage. The client states "After the first two pills, I thought I might as well enjoy myself and do two more." The assumption that more is better is a common one, and in this situation it actually appears to have led to the use of alcohol and sedatives in addition to the stimulants. Note that the idea might also underlie thoughts related to abstinence violation. The client essentially thought that the first two pills were some sort of study aid, but once those two had been consumed, subsequent pills were just for fun. Challenging thoughts like these can help clients avoid turning a little use into a lot.

This straightforward functional analysis revealed important targets for intervention related to multiple domains, including time management, social skills, social support, drug expectancies, and other maladaptive thoughts. It also provides valuable data for preventing relapse, teaching about abstinence violation, and demonstrating the impact of seemingly irrelevant decisions. The approach is ideally integrative and individualized in ways that clients are likely to find pertinent and helpful.

4.4.2   Mutual Help and Self-Help Groups

Self-help groups for drug problems are varied and numerous

People with substance abuse problems use self-help groups, particularly 12-step oriented ones like Alcoholics Anonymous and Narcotics Anonymous, more than formal treatment (Carrico et al., 2007). Nearly every person with a substance abuse problem has heard of these programs; many people connected to the addictions field have strong opinions about their own perceptions of the way these programs work. Mental health professionals also have a variety of opinions on 12-step programs that range from the devoted to the disdainful. In the US, the overwhelming majority of public substance abuse treatment programs rely heavily on 12-step groups, particularly the Department of Veteran's Affairs. Approximately 90% of private treatment centers also use 12-step approaches exclusively or as an adjunct to other treatments. Face-to-face meetings occur in thousands of communities worldwide and online meetings occur multiple times each day (http://www.aaonline.net). Some view the strength of the 12-step movements in the US as a blessing; others see it as cult-like (Peele, 2000).

Much of the initial evidence to support 12-step treatments was anecdotal. On nearly every evening in any large city in many countries, people speak in meetings who attribute their years of abstinence to the 12 steps. These happy outcomes met with some understandable skepticism from the research community. Because of the import of anonymity in the 12-step approach, long-term follow-up data on large samples were lacking, and no one had randomly assigned clients to treatment. Early studies included clients coerced into treatment, essentially violating one of the primary requirements for joining the 12-step fellowship – a desire to stop using drugs. These methodological problems made interpretation of the results of 12-step treatments impossible.

Investigations of 12-step treatments improved dramatically with large, randomized clinical trials (RCTs) that included the newly developed 12-step facilitation therapy (TSF; Nowinksi & Baker, 1998). TSF focuses on key concepts in the 12-step programs, encourages regular attendance and participation at meetings, finding a sponsor, and remaining active in the fellowship. TSF is certainly more than a simple recommendation to attend meetings. It has created impressive results and compares favorably to other popular therapeutic approaches, including motivational interviewing and cognitive-behavioral treatment.

An early investigation supported TSF's efficacy with alcohol dependent clients in a large multisite randomized control trial. At the time, Project MATCH (Matching Alcoholism Treatment to Heterogeneity) was the largest test of individual psychotherapies for any disorder. More than 1,700 participants received TSF, motivational interviews, or cognitive-behavioral therapy. Participants who received TSF showed the highest rates of abstinence. Given the consistent emphasis on abstinence in twelve-step programs, the result might not be a huge surprise. Those with the most severe alcohol dependence and those with the fewest psychiatric symptoms had better outcomes in TSF than in other treatments. These results confirmed that therapists could increase involvement in 12-step programs and create good outcomes by connecting alcohol-dependent clients to the fellowship (Project MATCH Research Group, 1997).

Extending this work to other drugs of abuse seemed an obvious next step. A similar RCT for cocaine dependence included almost 500 participants and found that a TSF treatment produced the best outcomes at 12-month follow-up.

This study revealed that consistent participation in 12-step activities improved outcomes more than simple attendance at meetings. Those who regularly spoke at meetings, helped at meetings in some way (e.g., making coffee, etc.), talked to a sponsor, read relevant literature, and worked on steps had better outcomes (Crits-Christoph et al., 1999; Weiss et al., 2005). These results helped extend previous work with alcohol to show that TSF could help abusers of an illicit drug, and confirmed that involvement in the fellowship appeared to lead to greater improvement.

Additional studies suggest that connecting clients to 12-step groups, even without all the components of TSF treatment, improves abstinence rates. One intriguing study showed that an intensive referral to a 12-step program produced greater rates of involvement and more abstinence than standard referrals (Timko & Debenedetti, 2007). The intensive referral included several components. The therapist provided clients with a list of meetings, meeting times, and directions, and reviewed a handout that explained many aspects of the 12-step approach. The therapist also introduced the client to an AA or NA volunteer, assessed attendance at meetings, and provided a list of recommended sponsors. Unsurprisingly, this approach led to increased attendance at meetings, more involvement, more reading of relevant literature, and a higher likelihood of obtaining a sponsor. In addition, the intensive referral led to more abstinence. Another study with a less elaborate intervention simply compared a treatment facility that had a 12-step program on site to one that did not. The one with the 12-step program on site led to better outcomes one year later, including more attendance at meetings and greater rates of abstinence. A single study like this one is hardly definitive, but it supports the idea that easy access to 12-step fellowship can enhance results (Laudet, Stanick, & Sands, 2007). Some of these results are so new that it is unclear how they will alter clinician behavior and 12-step participation.

Novel Components of 12-Step Facilitation (TSF)

The Individual Counseling Manual (Mercer & Woody, 1999), comparable to the one used in the randomized trial with cocaine-dependent clients, is available for free at the National Institute on Drug Abuse website: http://www.drugabuse.gov/TXManuals/IDCA/IDCA1.html.

A quick look reveals that approaches to assessment, relapse prevention, and the therapeutic relationship are remarkably similar to those used in motivational interviewing and cognitive behavioral therapy. These similarities may account for the comparable outcomes across different treatments seen in Project MATCH. Essential differences stem from a focus on connecting clients to a 12-step fellowship. A great deal of academic work suggests that differences between 12-step and other treatments arise from the disease model. The disease model presented in the manual may differ dramatically from many lay stereotypes about it. The model has become so controversial in some settings that arguments about it grow heated and convoluted. These arguments essentially depend on the definition of disease.

Viewing the disease model in historical context may prove helpful. AA has roots in The Oxford Group, a religious organization that had not focused exclusively on abstaining from alcohol, which became a haven for some problem drinkers in the 1920s and 1930s. Two members of The Oxford Group,

William Wilson (the legendary "Bill W.") and Robert Smith, founded AA in an effort to create a fellowship that focused exclusively on recovery and less on religion. At the time, treatments for alcohol problems were limited and often focused on moral weakness or lack of willpower. Conceptualizing alcoholism as a disease provided a liberating paradigm shift with the potential to limit destructive self-blame.

Although people with extensive experience in 12-step treatments might guffaw at the idea, many of the unique features of TSF do not rely on the disease model and are not closely linked to specific notions of spirituality. A great many regular participants in 12-step treatments hold the ideas of disease and spirituality rather lightly, making nuanced definitions of these terms less of a priority than their own sobriety. The TSF treatment focuses on regular attendance at meetings, active participation in the fellowship, making friends who support abstinence, regularly reading 12-step material, working the steps, and finding a sponsor. Regular attendance at meetings is operationalized in the treatment manual as three times per week, though many 12-step programs strongly encourage daily attendance in the initial stages of treatment. Contrary to popular belief, the AA "Big Book" mentions meetings only rarely and makes no recommendations about daily attendance. Participation begins as a recommendation to speak during at least one meeting per week, with the hope that speaking will lead to greater involvement like helping out in the preparation of meetings.

Note that these behaviors are all essentially incompatible with drug use, making improvement consistent with behavioral theories of choice (Correia, 2005). The extensive investment of time and effort in the recovery process also may make relapse less likely in ways that are consistent with cognitive dissonance theory (Festinger, 1961). Clients may find themselves thinking, "I just went to all these meetings, read this Big Book, and worked all these steps, I must really want to stay drug-free." Speaking up in meetings is identical to the public commitment common in motivational interviewing and guided self-change approaches. Making friends in the fellowship and finding a sponsor is also consistent with many models of social support. Thus, 12-step programs likely work in multiple ways, much like other treatments. Several alternative approaches that rely on self- and mutual-help techniques have also developed. Most have less of an emphasis on spiritual aspects of recovery but may work via other mechanisms.

Alternative Self- and Mutual-Help Approaches

Alternative approaches have developed for clients or clinicians who find aspects of the 12-step program unworkable. Three popular programs include Secular Organization for Sobriety (SOS), Rational Recovery, as well as Self-Management and Recovery Training (SMART). Empirical support for these programs is less extensive than the research related to 12-step programs. Nevertheless, initial results show promise and some aspects of these approaches parallel empirically validated cognitive behavior therapy.

Secular Organization for Sobriety

Secular Organization for Sobriety (SOS), as its name implies, presents itself as an alternative to spiritually focused treatments. It is also known as Save

Our Selves (SOS), in reference to its emphasis on individual responsibility for avoiding lapses. SOS includes regular meetings, which it holds throughout the US and in some other countries. The program makes sobriety an individual's top priority and separates this issue from all others, including religious and spiritual ones. It recommends self-identifying as an addict and appreciating the social support of others in recovery in ways that parallel the 12-step approach.

Rational Recovery

Rational Recovery at one time held self-help meetings but now views them as counterproductive. The program is primarily educational and focuses on cognitive-behavioral techniques, particularly those linked to rational emotive behavior therapy (Ellis, 1969). Many of the tenets of Rational Recovery are conspicuously counter to 12-step ideas. The program views meetings as an indirect way to justify using drugs when social support is unavailable. It emphasizes that "you are on your own," and actively disputes ideas like denial, powerlessness, and "one-day-at-time" approaches. Participants essentially decide that they will never use drugs again and that they will not change their mind about the decision.

The program currently focuses on the idea of the "addiction voice," which includes any thoughts that encourage maladaptive drug use or addictive behaviors. Rational Recovery theory links this addiction voice loosely to limbic brain areas and labels it "the beast." A primary contributor to improvement involves the addiction voice recognition technique, which appears to rely on identifying thoughts and urges that arise from the addiction voice. Participants in the program can learn to identify thoughts and urges that arise from the addiction voice so that they can dispute or accept them in a way that does not lead to substance use. As unorthodox as some of this material may sound, it shares an idea related to current work on acceptance and mindfulness-based treatments. If clients can identify certain thoughts as the voice of the beast, they need not act on these thoughts so much as see them for mental events that do not have to determine behavior. The approach may not require disputing the thoughts directly or creating any internal conflict so much as distancing one's identity and actions from these powerless cognitions.

Self-Management and Recovery Training

Self-Management and Recovery Training (SMART) grew out of Rational Recovery. SMART recovery relies on many standard cognitive behavioral techniques, particularly those common to Ellis's rational emotive behavior therapy (Ellis, 1969). For example, Ellis's ABC conceptualization of the role of cognition in determining affect and behavior is central to the treatment. Client readings include training in disputing irrational or maladaptive cognitions. The program has incorporated the Stages of Change Model (despite some of the drawbacks mentioned above), includes cost/benefit analyses comparable to the decisional balance intervention in motivational interviewing, and addresses negative affect and cues for drug use in ways that are consistent with cognitive behavioral models. SMART recovery has face-to-face meetings (though fewer than the 12-step programs) and online meetings. A trained facilitator who has maintained sobriety or never experienced addiction problems runs meetings. These meetings generally focus on enhancing motivation for abstinence, coping with urges to use, solving problems, and balancing short and long-term desires. SMART recovery does not view itself as incompatible with 12-step approaches, but sidesteps the issues of spirituality, denial, and disease. An intriguing study comparing SMART recovery and a 12-step program for dually diagnosed clients found some advantages for each approach. Clients improved in both treatments. The 12-step approach led to less alcohol and marijuana consumption and more social interactions; the SMART recovery program created greater improvements in employment and health (Brooks & Penn, 2003).

Working with clients who are interested in affiliating with these organizations requires some of the same strategies used in 12-step facilitation. Ensuring that they are connected to the association, participating in an active way, and monitoring progress can communicate an important interest in the strategy, allow the clients to detail which aspects they find most helpful, and provide an opportunity to supplement this work with empirically supported techniques. Popular self-help groups related to drug use include: Narcotics Anonymous (NA, http://www.na.org/), Cocaine Anonymous (CA, http://www.ca.org), Secular Organization for Sobriety (SOS, http://www.secularsobriety.org), Rational Recovery (RR, http://www.rational.org), and Self-Management and Recovery Training (SMART, http://www.smartrecovery.org).

4.4.3   Meditation Techniques.

Meditation techniques have become a part of many treatments for a host of physiological and psychological problems, including addiction to drugs. Meditation lacks the potential stigma associated with treatments specifically focused on drug problems, and costs considerably less than many alternatives. Data using a number of different outcomes reveal that meditation does not produce the same results as simple relaxation, suggesting that relaxation is not the lone mechanism behind its results. Treatments for drug problems have successfully incorporated either key ideas from meditation or direct meditation practices as a component. The mechanisms behind the decreases in drug use remain unclear.

Most meditation techniques include aspects of relaxation, concentration, and acceptance. Theorists suggest that the relaxation component decreases stress, making it ideal for those who use drugs to reduce tension. The concentration component may increase mental clarity. Improved mental clarity could help a number of daily tasks, and certainly assist participants when they make decisions to avoid problematic use of drugs. The acceptance component emphasizes that denying negative emotions, cumbersome situations, and personal problems proves more difficult than acknowledging their existence. Acceptance does not mean that clients should endure unacceptable predicaments, and may correspond to the same idea common in 12-step approaches. This form of acceptance rests on the idea that recognizing the reality of a situation is essential before deciding on a course of action. This acceptance enables participants to understand that craving, urges, withdrawal, and negative affect are a part of everyday experience that need not lead to drug use. Although meditation techniques come in numerous varieties, only two have received relevant empirical investigation: Transcendental and Vipassana (Mindfulness).

Transcendental Meditation (TM) has improved problem drinking in at least two studies. TM is not part of a religion, philosophy, or belief system. The technique defies easy, written explanation, but includes the effortless use of a mantra. Practitioners of the technique consider the mantra a sound vibration that the participant experiences in the mind without exerting effort to generate it. By design, the vibration encourages the slowing of thought, a gradual focus on the mantra alone, and an eventual decrease of all thoughts. Clients practice the technique twice a day for 20 minutes at a time. In truth, organizing a schedule to incorporate this daily technique would undoubtedly improve the lives of many. Only certified instructors can provide training in the technique; classes occur regularly in many large cities in the US and around the world. The current training program requires up to two hours of instruction on four occasions as well as a nominal fee (see http://www.tm.org).

Mindfulness Meditation, sometimes called Vipassana meditation, is a technique that encourages focus on bodily sensations (particularly the breath), letting thoughts pass as they are recognized as *just* thoughts. The technique emphasizes accepting stimuli for what they really are, as they occur, and has helped incarcerated men and women decrease their drug and alcohol use in a large study (Bowen et al., 2006). Though it is not a religious practice, it is rooted in Buddhist principles that chiefly see the cause of suffering as the result of not seeing events accurately. Vipassana directly reflects this principle, loosely translated as "seeing things as they are." Participants in Bowen and colleagues (2006) investigation learned the technique during a 10-day session that included multiple hours of meditation per day, refraining from writing, limiting speaking, and eating a vegetarian diet (all aspects of a focus on lifestyle change rather than symptom-based change). The course is free of charge at a number of centers located throughout the world as well as in rented space in many more cities (see http://www.dhamma.org). Data from the study on drug use in prisoners suggest that those participating in the meditation experience were less likely to try to avoid their own thoughts, which accounted for part of the impact of the treatment on alcohol consumption (Bowen et al., 2007). Perhaps the acceptance of thoughts, even uncomfortable ones related to drug use, as well as the promotion of lifestyle change underlies the impact of meditation on these outcomes.

Mindfulness-Based Stress Reduction (MBSR; Kabat-Zinn, 2003) integrates components from Vipassana style meditation and cognitive behavioral stress reduction. Similar to the program of Bowen and colleagues (2006), the emphasis is on acceptance of thoughts, body sensation, and emotion. Mindfulness refers to the conscious awareness of the current moment, recognizing that this is a continuous and sometimes arduous process. Attending to what is happening right here and right now is essential. Regular practice can increase recognition of bodily sensations as well as insight into the chatter that often occurs within the mind. The increased recognition of bodily sensations can help practitioners notice cravings and urges as well as subtle cues of tension and emotional arousal. Insight into the ubiquitous chatter of the mind allows practitioners to notice that thoughts often reflect a distortion of reality, which is in some ways remarkably similar to aspects of cognitive behavioral therapy. The practice of mindfulness is divided into formal and informal. Formal practice essentially consists of sitting quietly with the aim of intentionally paying attention to present moment experience. Informal practice consists of using present moment awareness to recognize subtle aspects of normal daily activities (e.g., walking). Participants can learn mindfulness meditation by formally taking an MBSR course (http://www.umassmed.edu/cfm/mbsr/) or by accessing books or guided recordings (http://www.mindfulnesstapes.com). Recorded meditations range from 10 to 45 minutes. Formal MBSR programs typically require 8-12 weekly sessions, as well as committed individual practice, though more brief adaptations (4 weeks) of this program have been employed in some research paradigms. The MBSR program has not been directly linked to drug abuse but shows promise for general stress and related disorders (see Grossman et al., 2004).

4.4.4   Psychopharmacological Adjuncts to Treatment

Pharmacological treatments can help improve relapse rates

A few medications have been approved for the treatment of drug-related or alcohol disorders (Montoya & Vocci, 2008). All have some empirical support for their utility in that they perform better than a placebo for helping clients maintain abstinence. The medications invariably work best in conjunction with psychotherapy. Although the idea of using one drug in an effort to refrain from using another strikes some members of the treatment community as illogical, the approach is consistent with the biological aspect of the biopsychosocial model. The idea also aligns with harm reduction, as these medications have few side effects and none of the negative consequences associated with psychoactive drug abuse. These programs require close supervision by a physician. Drugs approved for treatment of dependence in some countries include naloxone, methadone, buprenorphine, levo-α-acetylmethadol (LAAM), acamprosate, and disulfiram.

Pharmacotherapy has considerable intuitive appeal for opiate dependence. Opiates tend to create rapid tolerance, aversive withdrawal, and a high risk for relapse, making the potential gain from a medical intervention that supplements psychotherapy very attractive. One approach to opiate pharmacotherapy relies on an opiate antagonist (naloxone or naltrexone), which blocks opiate receptors and the effects of the abusable drugs. Other forms of pharmacotherapy rely on opiate agonists or partial agonists, those that stimulate the same receptors. These tend to minimize withdrawal, craving, and the subjective effects of injected opiates of abuse (methadone, buprenorphine, and LAAM).

Naloxone and naltrexone block opiate receptors, essentially eliminating any reinforcing effects of subsequent opiate administration. These drugs may reduce craving for opiates as well. In addition, both have also helped clients stay away from alcohol. Given the high comorbidity of alcohol and opiate-related problems, this extra effect could be a bonus. Methadone, the most frequently used opiate therapy for heroin dependence, requires the daily administration of a prescribed dose. It decreases psychosocial and medical complications, reduces consumption of opiate drugs, and can lessen other risky behaviors (Draper & McCance-Katz, 2005). Methadone is an opiate itself but one that does not create the infamous rush of subjective euphoria associated with other opiates, even when injected. Although the intensity of the response to the drug is minimal, its duration is markedly longer than heroin or morphine's. Thus, methadone essentially combines with opiate receptors in a way that eases withdrawal and craving from other opiates. In addition, an injection of other opiate drugs will not have its usual dramatic impact if methadone is already present at the receptor. These qualities help methadone decrease withdrawal symptoms and rates of relapse. Nevertheless, because it is an opiate, methadone has abuse potential itself, particularly at higher doses (Julien, 2005).

Buprenorphine, a drug with partial agonist and antagonist properties, stimulates one type of opiate receptor somewhat, but less than opiate drugs of abuse like morphine or heroin. It also antagonizes another opiate receptor, enhancing its potential to decrease relapse. Treatment outcome studies generally reveal that buprenorphine performs as well as methadone. It may have less abuse potential than methadone, as additional doses seem to create sadness and fatigue rather than euphoria (Singhal, Tripathi, Pal, Jena, & Jain,, 2007). Buprenorphine is also available in combination with naloxone, further decreasing its abuse potential. Because it is not an opiate like methadone, office-based physicians can prescribe it, and take-home supplies for multiple days of treatment are available. Buprenorphine lacks the stigma associated with methadone.

LAAM is an opiate drug comparable to methadone. LAAM has an advantage over methadone because its longer duration of action eliminates the need to administer it daily. Administration three times per week appears sufficient. At least one study found LAAM superior to methadone for maintaining abstinence from other opiate drugs, but LAAM may be less effective than methadone for treatment retention (Anglin et al., 2007). Physicians tend to prescribe LAAM only after methadone or buprenorphine have failed. It is not approved for use in Canada.

Pharmacotherapies for stimulant abuse and dependence have not shown as much promise as those used for problems with the opiates. No drug has received regulatory approval for cocaine dependence. A series of studies suggests that stimulant drugs administered orally at low doses have the potential to improve outcomes for a subset of cocaine-dependent clients (Castells et al., 2007) A few drugs have decreased craving for cocaine in the laboratory but have yet to improve outcomes for cocaine-dependent clients in treatment. One pilot study administered methylphenidate (Ritalin) to cocaine-dependent clients with attention deficit disorder and improved their outcomes. Exciting new work using levodopa, a precursor to dopamine (the neurotransmitter affected by cocaine), suggests it can improve cocaine abstinence rates when used in conjunction with a contingency management program that rewards clean urine screens. Nevertheless, excessive dopamine can create aversive side effects (Karila et al., 2008). Crack cocaine smokers given Modafinil, a stimulant-like medication used in the treatment of narcolepsy, smoked less cocaine and found its subjective effects less intense in the laboratory over 48 days of trials, suggesting it should help treatment outcome (Hart, Haney, Vosburg, Rubin, & Foltin, 2008).

Dronabinol, a synthetic form of the active ingredient in marijuana (THC), unsurprisingly decreases withdrawal from smoked marijuana and has helped treatment in two case studies (Levin & Kleber, 2008). Using THC to treat marijuana dependence met with guffaws and chagrin in some circles, but the rationale for the approach concerns the difference between orally administered and smoked drugs. The synthetic THC pill has a gradual onset of effects. At low doses the impact on mood would be less dramatic than smoked marijuana. Clients might find tapering off of the orally administered doses easier than decreasing consumption of smoked marijuana. Nevertheless, the potential for abuse of such a drug remains.

Two medications that target alcohol dependence are worth mentioning here. Alcohol dependence and other substance use disorders covary dramatically. In addition, alcohol intoxication can increase the chance of a return to inappropriate use of other drugs. Thus, some clients who use other drugs problematically may benefit from abstaining from alcohol. Disulfiram interferes with alcohol metabolism; drinking after taking this medication leads to aversive flushing, nausea, and other uncomfortable physical reactions. As one might guess, the medication only works when taken. Despite its legendary reputation and decades of use, research suggests outcomes vary dramatically, with some studies showing no advantage for those taking disulfiram unless they are remarkably motivated and compliant (Kenna, Nielsen, Wello, Schiesl, & Swift, 2007). Acamprosate, a drug that appears to work in the glutamate neurotransmitter system, improves length of time until relapse for alcoholics. It may work particularly well for clients who drink alcohol in an effort to relieve withdrawal (Mann, Kiefer, Spanagel, & Littleton, 2008). These combinations of pharmacological and psychological interventions have considerable potential for improving treatment outcome.

4.5   Multicultural Issues

Optimal assessments and treatments might vary with gender, ethnicity, age, and other factors

Optimal assessment and treatment for drug problems might differ for clients of different age, gender, and ethnicity. Research reveals that items designed to assess specific troubles or diagnostic symptoms may mean different things to different people. Established scales may require different cut-offs for different groups. Some scales simply may not measure the same construct in men and women (Lavender, Looby, & Earleywine, 2008), different ethnic groups (Schroeder & Moolchan, 2007), or younger and older clients (Chen & Anthony, 2003). An example from the marijuana literature may help explain this phenomenon. Among men and women who report comparable levels of marijuana-related problems, the men are more likely to report problems with their partners. Among heterosexual couples, women may be more likely than men to express concerns or complaints to a partner about their cannabis use. Perhaps women choose to raise concerns with a partner at a lower problem severity threshold than would be required for men to raise similar concerns (Lavender et al., 2008). These results underscore the point that follow-up discussions with clients about assessment results are essential. The use of these scales in treatment must keep these gender differences in mind.

Developmental changes can interfere with accurate assessment of drug-related problems in adolescents, but researchers have made considerable progress on specific assessment devices and treatments for this population. Adolescent versions of many problem scales tend to emphasize domains more salient to this period of development, including conflict with parents and family, problems in school (rather than at work), and items related to peers and dating (rather than marriage). Despite the extensive literature on adolescents, work in the elderly, women, and in different ethnic groups lags. These gaps in the literature should receive attention in coming years. Regardless, an ideographic approach to the role of drugs in each client's optimal functioning can be invaluable to individual interventions. A few minutes spent discussing the meaning of specific items or questions is time well spent. Ideographic adjustments to interventions that focus on motivation, cognitions, and skills can help individual clinicians adapt empirically supported treatments to each client. Ideally, a good functional analysis and warm therapeutic relationship has the potential to help clients of any ethnic group, gender, age, or sexual orientation. Nevertheless, consulting with experts on these groups (including members who are eager to talk) can provide valuable insights into how to optimize the functional analysis and the relationship.

Further Readings

Denning, P. (2004). *Practicing harm reduction psychotherapy: An alternative approach to addictions*. New York: Guilford.

This book begins with a great review of the conceptual foundations of harm reduction and emphasizes the empirical support for the approach. It then moves to practical, intuitive, and flexible recommendations for working with clients who wish to explore abstinence and other treatment goals.

Donovan, D. & Marlatt, G. A. *Assessment of Addictive Behaviors* (2nd ed.). New York: Guilford.

This book contains state of the art assessment devices and approaches for nearly every drug and addictive behavior. Each chapter stands alone nicely, making it an easy, accessible reference.

Marlatt, G. A. (2002). *Harm reduction: Pragmatic strategies for managing high-risk behaviors*. New York: Guilford.

Marlatt begins with detailed chapters on the history and strategies of harm reduction. Subsequent edited chapters by world authorities address increasing the safety of drugs of all types, minimizing risky sexual behavior, tailoring interventions to special populations, and taking steps to improve public policy.

Miller, W. R., & Rollnick, S. (2002). *Motivational interviewing: Preparing people for change*. New York: Guilford.

This classic text on motivational interviewing begins with detailed and accessible explanations of all the key components of the treatment and easy ways to learn them. A subsequent edited section provides perspectives from multiple authors on a range of topics, including applications to special populations and work in groups. The first edition (1992) had a different set of edited chapters and is also valuable.

Nowinksi, J., & Baker, S. (1998). *The twelve-step facilitation handbook: A systematic approach to early recovery from alcoholism and addiction*. New York: Josey-Bass.

An intriguing and enthusiastic manual for conducting sessions designed to connect clients to the 12-step fellowship, get them to become active participants, and help them maintain sobriety. Special sections focus on central concepts, including denial, enabling, surrender, and codependency. This text also reviews the outcome data from Project Match that support the efficacy of the treatment.

Rotgers, F., Morgenstern, J., & Walters, S. (2006). *Treating substance abuse: Theory and technique* (2nd ed.). New York: Guilford.

Experts present alternating chapters on theory and technique that address twelve-step, family, psychoanalytic, cognitive behavioral, and a host of other approaches to treating problem drug use.

Sobell, M. B., & Sobell, L. C. (1996). *Problem drinkers: Guided self-change treatment*. New York: Guilford.

This practical, structured, empirically-supported book walks clients and therapists through the step-by-step process for overcoming alcohol-related problems in clear, accessible language. The text contains all the forms, hand-outs, and illustrations a client could ever need, and they adapt easily to any drug of abuse and a range of other problem behaviors.

6

References

Adamson, S. J., & Sellman, J. D. (2001). Drinking goal selection and treatment outcome in out-patients with mild-moderate alcohol dependence. *Drug and Alcohol Review, 20,* 351–359.

Adinoff, B. (2004). Neurobiologic processes in drug reward and addiction. *Harvard Review of Psychiatry, 12,* 305–320.

Agrawal, A., & Lynskey, M. T. (2008). Are there genetic influences on addiction: Evidence from family, adoption and twin studies. *Addiction, 103,* 1069–1081.

Alexander, D., & Leung, P. (2006). The Marijuana Screening Inventory (MSI-X): concurrent, convergent and discriminant validity with multiple measures. *The American Journal of Drug and Alcohol Abuse, 32,* 351–378.

American Psychiatric Association. (1994). *Diagnostic and statistical manual of mental disorders* (4th ed.). Washington, DC: Author.

Anderson, D. A., Simmons, A. M., Martens, M. P., Ferrier, A. G., & Sheehy, M. J. (2006). The relationship between disordered eating behavior and drinking motives in college-age women. *Eating Behaviors, 7,* 419–422.

Anglin, M. D., Conner, B. T., Annon, J., & Longshore, D. (2007). Levo-alpha-acetylmethadol (LAAM) versus methadone maintenance: 1-year treatment retention, outcomes and status. *Addiction, 102,* 1432–1442.

Bandura, A. (1977). Self-efficacy: Toward a unifying theory of behavioral change. *Psychological Review, 84,* 191–215.

Beck, J. S., Liese, B. S., & Najavits, L. M. (2005). Cognitive therapy. In R. J. Frances, S. I. Miller, & A. H. Mack (Eds.), *Clinical textbook of addictive disorders* (3rd ed.) (pp. 474–501). New York: Guilford Press.

Becker, J. B., & Hu, M. (2008). Sex differences in drug abuse. *Frontiers in Neuroendocrinology, 29,* 36–47.

Biener, L., & Abrams, D. (1991). The Contemplation Ladder: Validation of a measure of readiness to consider smoking cessation. *Health Psychology, 10,* 360–365.

Bjornaas, M. A., Bekken, A. S., Ojlert, A., Haldorsen, T., Jacobsen, D., Rostrup, M., & Ekeberg, O. (2008). A 20-year prospective study of mortality and causes of death among hospitalized opioid addicts in Oslo. *BMC Psychiatry, 8,* 1–8.

Black, W. D. (2007). Antisocial personality disorder, conduct disorder, and psychopathy. In J. E. Grant & M. N. Potenza (Eds.), *Textbook of men's mental health* (pp. 143–170). Arlington, VA: American Psychiatric Publishing, Inc.

Bornovalova, M. A., & Daughters, S. B. (2007). How does dialectical behavior therapy facilitate treatment retention among individuals with comorbid borderline personality disorder and substance use disorders? *Clinical Psychology Review, 27,* 923–943.

Bowen, S., Witkiewitz, K., Dillworth, T. M., Chawla, N., Simpson, T. L., Ostafin, B. D., Larimer, M. E., Blume, A. W., Parks, G. A., Marlatt, G. A. (2006). Mindfulness mediation and substance use in an incarcerated population. *Psychology of Addictive Behaviors, 20,* 343–347.

Bowen, S., Witkiewitz, K., Dillworth, T. M., & Marlatt, G. A. (2007). The role of thought suppression in the relationship between mindfulness mediation and alcohol use. *Addictive Behaviors, 32,* 2324–2328.

Brooks, A. J., & Penn, P. E. (2003). Comparing treatments for dual diagnosis: Twelve-step and Self-Management and Recovery Training. *American Journal of Drug and Alcohol Abuse, 29,* 359–383.

Buckland, P. R. (2008). Will we ever find the genes for addiction? *Addiction, 103*, 1768–1776.

Carey, K. B., Purnine, D. M., Maisto, S. A., & Carey, M. (1999). Assessing readiness to change substance abuse: A critical review of instruments. *Clinical Psychology: Science and Practice, 6*, 245–266.

Carrico, A. W., Gifford, E. V., & Moos, R. H. (2007). Spirituality/religiosity promotes acceptance-based responding and 12-step involvement. *Drug and Alcohol Dependence, 89,* 66–73.

Castells, X., Casas, M., Vidal, X., Bosch, R., Roncero, C., Ramos-Quiroga, J. A., & et al. (2007). Efficacy of central nervous system stimulant treatment for cocaine dependence: a systematic review and meta-analysis of randomized controlled clinical trials. *Addiction, 102,* 1871–1887.

Chen, C., & Anthony, J. C. (2003). Possible age-associated bias in reporting of clinical features of drug dependence: Epidemiological evidence on adolescent-onset marijuana use. *Addiction, 98,* 71–82.

Clayton, R. R., Segress, M. J., & Caudill, C. A. (2008). Prevention of substance abuse. In M. Galanter & H. D. Kleber (Eds.), *The American Psychiatric Publishing textbook of substance abuse treatment* (4th ed.) (pp. 681–688). Arlington, VA: American Psychiatric Publishing.

Compton, W. M., Thomas, Y. F., Stinson, F. S., & Grant, B. F. (2007). Prevalence, correlates, disability, and comorbidity of DSM-IV drug abuse and dependence in the United States: Results from the national epidemiologic survey on alcohol and related conditions. *Archives of General Psychiatry, 64,* 566–576.

Comtois, K. A., & Linehan, M. M. (2006). Psychosocial treatments of suicidal behaviors: A practice-friendly review. *Journal of Clinical Psychology, 62,* 161–170.

Copeland, J., Gilmour, S., Gates, P., & Swift, W. (2005). The Cannabis Problems Questionnaire: Factor structure, reliability, and validity. *Drug and Alcohol Dependence, 80,* 313–319.

Correia, C. (2005). Behavioral theories of choice. In M. Earleywine (Ed.), *Mind-altering drugs: The science of subjective experience* (pp. 3–24). New York: Oxford University Press.

Crits-Christoph, P., Siqueland, L., Blaine, J., Frank, A., Luborsky, L., Onken, L. S., et al. (1999). Psychosocial treatments for cocaine dependence: National Institute on Drug Abuse Collaborative Cocaine Treatment Study. *Archives of General Psychiatry, 56,* 493–502.

Davis, L., Uezato, A., Newell, J. M., & Frazier, E. (2008). Major depression and comorbid substance use disorders. *Current Opinion in Psychiatry, 21,* 14–18.

de Bruijn, C., Korzec, A., Koerselman, F., & van den Brink, W. (2004). Craving and withdrawal as core symptoms of alcohol dependence. *The Journal of Nervous and Mental Disease, 192,* 494–502.

Degenhardt, L., Chiu, W. T., Sampson, N., Kessler, R. C., Anthony, J. C., Angermeyer, M., et al. (2008). Toward a global view of alcohol, tobacco, cannabis, and cocaine use: Findings from the WHO World Mental Health Surveys. *PLoS Med, 5*, 141.

Denning, P. (2004). *Practicing harm reduction psychotherapy: An alternative approach to addictions.* New York: Guilford.

Denning, P., Little, J., & Glickman, A. (2004). *Over the influence: The harm reduction guide for managing drugs and alcohol.* New York: Guilford Press.

Denson, T., & Earleywine, M. (2006). Pot-head or pot smoker? A taxometric investigation of cannabis dependence. *Substance Abuse Treatment, Prevention, and Policy, 1,* 22. Available online at http://www.substanceabusepolicy.com/content/1/1/22

Department of Health and Human Services. (2007). *National household survey on drug abuse: Population estimates, 2006.* Washington, DC: U.S. Government Printing Office.

Devaney, M. L., Reid, G., & Baldwin, S. (2007). Prevalence of illicit drug use in Asia and the Pacific. *Drug and Alcohol Review, 26,* 97–102.

Donovan, D. M., & Marlatt, G. A. (Eds.). (2008). *Assessment of addictive behaviors* (2nd ed.). New York: Guilford Press.

Draper, J. C., & McCance-Katz, E. F. (2005). Medical illness and comorbidities in drug users: Implications for addiction pharmacotherapy treatment. *Substance Use and Misuse, 40,* 1899–1921.

Earleywine, M. (Ed.) (2005). *Mind-altering drugs: The science of subjective experience.* New York: Oxford University Press.

Elkins, I. J., McGue, M., & Iacono, W. G. (2007). Prospective effects of attention-deficit/hyperactivity disorder, conduct disorder, and sex on adolescent substance use and abuse. *Archives of General Psychiatry, 64,* 1145–1152.

Ellis, A. (1969). Rational-emotive therapy. *Journal of Contemporary Psychotherapy, 1,* 82–90.

Fendrich, M., Mackesy-Amiti, M. E., Johnson, T. P., Hubbell, A., & Wislar, J. (2005). Tobacco-reporting validity in an epidemiological drug-use survey. *Addictive Behaviors, 30,* 175–181.

Festinger, L. (1961). The psychological effects of insufficient rewards. *American Psychologist, 16,* 1–11.

First, M. B., Spitzer, R. L., Gibbon M., & Williams, J. B. W. (1996). *Structured Clinical Interview for DSM-IV Axis I Disorders, Clinician Version (SCID-CV).* Washington, DC: American Psychiatric Press, Inc.

Flynn, P. M., & Brown, B. S. (2008). Co-occurring disorders in substance abuse treatment: Issues and prospects. *Journal of Substance Abuse Treatment, 34,* 36–47.

Gadalla, T., & Piran, N. (2007). Co-occurrence of eating disorders and alcohol use disorders in women: A meta-analysis. *Archives of Women's Mental Health, 10,* 133–140.

Gallerani, M., Manfredini, R., Dal Monte, D., Calò, G., Brunaldi, V., & Simonato, M. (2001) Circadian differences in the individual sensitivity to opiate overdose. *Critical Care Medicine, 29,* 96–101.

Gore, R., & Earleywine, M. (2007). Marijuana's perceived addictiveness: A survey of clinicians and researchers. In M. Earleywine (Ed.), *Pot politics: The cost of prohibition* (pp. 176–188). New York: Oxford University Press.

Grant, B. F., Compton, W. M., Crowley, T. J., Hasin, D. S., Helzer, J. E., Li, T. K., at al. (2007). Errors in assessing DSM-IV substance use disorders. *Archives of General Psychiatry, 64,* 379–380.

Grant, B. F., Stinson, F. S., Dawson, D. A., Chou, S. P., Dufour, M. C., Compton, W., et al. (2004). Prevalence and co-occurrence of substance use disorders and independent mood and anxiety disorders: Results from the National Epidemiologic Survey on alcohol and related conditions. *Archives of General Psychiatry, 61,* 807–816.

Grossman, P. Niemann, L, Schmidt, S., & Walach, H. (2004). Mindfulness-based stress reduction and health benefits: A meta-analysis. *Journal of Psychosomatic Research, 57,* 35–43

Harris, E. C., & Barraclough, B. (1997). Suicide as an outcome for mental disorders. A meta-analysis. *The British Journal of Psychiatry: the Journal of Mental Science, 170,* 205–228.

Hart, C. L., Haney, M., Vosburg, S. K., Rubin, E., & Foltin, R. W. (2008). Smoked cocaine self-administration is decreased by modafinil. *Neuropsychopharmacology, 33,* 761–768.

Hasin, D., Samet, S., Nunes, E., Meydan, J., Matseoane, K., & Waxman, R. (2006). Diagnosis of comorbid psychiatric disorders in substance users assessed with the Psychiatric Research Interview for Substance and Mental Disorders for DSM-IV. *The American Journal of Psychiatry, 163,* 689–696.

Heyman, G. M. (1996). Resolving the contradictions of addiction. *Behavioral and Brain Sciences, 19,* 561–610.

Hicks, B. M., Blonigen, D. M., Kramer, M. D., Krueger, R. F., Patrick, C. J., Iacono, W. G., et al. (2007). Gender differences and developmental change in externalizing disorders from late adolescence to early adulthood: A longitudinal twin study. *Journal of Abnormal Psychology, 116,* 433–447.

Hser, Y. I., Longshore, D., & Anglin, M. D. (2007). The life course perspective on drug use: A conceptual framework for understanding drug use trajectories. *Evaluation Review, 31,* 515–547.

Ishikawa, S. S., & Raine, A. (2003). Prefrontal deficits and antisocial behavior: A causal model. In B. Lahey, T. E. Moffit, & A. Caspi (Eds.), *Causes of conduct disorder and juvenile delinquency* (pp. 277–304). New York: Guilford Press.

Janis, I. L., & Mann, L. (1977). *Decision making: A psychological analysis of conflict, choice, and commitment.* New York: Free Press.

Julien, R. M. (2005). *A primer of drug action: A comprehensive guide to the actions, uses, and side effects of psychoactive drugs* (10th ed.). New York: Worth Publishers.

Jungerman, F. S., Andreoni, S., & Laranjeira, R. (2007). Short term impact of same intensity but different duration interventions for cannabis users. *Drug and Alcohol Dependence, 90,* 120–127.

Kabat-Zinn, J. (2003). Mindfulness-based interventions in context: Past, present, and future. *Clinical Psychology: Science and Practice, 10,* 144–156.

Karila, L, Gorelick, D., Weinstein A., Noble, F., Benyamina, A., Coscas, S., et al. (2008). New treatments for cocaine dependence: A focused review. *The International Journal of Neuropsychopharmacology, 11,* 425–438.

Kenna, G. A., Nielsen, D. M., Mello, P., Schiesl, A., & Swift, R. M. (2007). Pharmacotherapy of dual substance abuse and dependence. *CNS Drugs, 21,* 213–237.

Kerr, D., Dietze, P., Kelly, A. M., & Jolley, D. (2008). Attitudes of Australian heroin users to peer distribution of naloxone for heroin overdose: Perspectives on intranasal administration. *Journal of Urban Health, 85,* 352–360.

Kessler, R. C., & Wang, P. S. (2008). The descriptive epidemiology of commonly occurring mental disorders in the United States. *Annual Review of Public Health, 29,* 115–129.

King, M. K., & Tucker, J. A. (2000). Behavior change patterns and strategies distinguishing moderation drinking and abstinence during the natural resolution of alcohol problems without treatment. *Psychology of Addictive Behaviors, 14,* 48–55.

Kirisci, L., Tarter, R., Mezzich, A., & Reynolds, M. (2008). Screening current and future diagnosis of psychiatric disorders using the Revised Drug Use Screening Inventory. *The American Journal of Drug and Alcohol Abuse, 34,* 653–665.

Klingemann, H. K., & Sobell, L. C. (2007). *Promoting self-change from addictive behaviors: Practical implications for policy, prevention, and treatment.* New York: Springer.

LaBrie, J. W., & Earleywine, M. (2003). Part I: Socially undesirable behaviors: The case of risky sex and drinking. *Sex Offender Law Report, 4,* 49–50, 59–62.

LaBrie, J., Quinlan, T. Schiffman, J., & Earleywine, M. (2005). Performance of alcohol and safer sex change rulers compared with readiness to change questionnaires. *Psychology of Addictive Behaviors, 19,* 11–115.

Laudet, A., Stanick, V., & Sands, B. (2007). An exploration of the effect of on-site 12-step meetings on post-treatment outcomes among polysubstance-dependent outpatient clients. *Evaluation Review, 31,* 613–646.

Lavender, J., Looby, A., & Earleywine, M. (2008). A brief Cannabis-Associated Problems Questionnaire with less potential for bias. *Human Psychopharmacology, 23,* 487–493.

Ledgerwood, D. M., Goldberger, B. A., Risk, N. K., Lewis, C. E., & Price, R. K. (2008). Comparison between self-report and hair analysis of illicit drug use in community sample of middle-aged men. *Addictive Behaviors, 33,*1131–1139.

Levin, F. R., & Kleber, H. D. (2008). Use of dronabinol for cannabis dependence: Two case reports and review. *The American Journal on Addictions, 17,* 161–164.

Linehan, M. M. (1993).*Cognitive-behavioral treatment of borderline personality disorder.* New York: Guilford Press.

Littrell, J. H., & Girvin, H. (2002). Stages of change: A critique. *Behavior Modification, 26,* 223–273.

Looby, A. (2008). Childhood attention deficit hyperactivity disorder and the development of substance use disorders: valid concern or exaggeration? *Addictive Behaviors, 33,* 451–463.

Luce, K. H., Engler, P. A., & Crowther, J. H. (2007). Eating disorders and alcohol use: Group differences in consumption rates and drinking motives. *Eating Behaviors, 8,* 177–184.

Lyvers, M. (2000). "Loss of control" in alcoholism and drug addiction: A neuroscientific interpretation. *Experimental and Clinical Psychopharmacology, 8,* 225–249.

Mann, K., Kiefer, F., Spanagel, R., & Littleton, J. (2008). Acamprosate: Recent findings and future research directions. *Alcoholism, Clinical and Experimental Research, 32,* 1105–1110.

Marissen, M., Franken, I., Blanken, P., van den Brink, W. & Hendriks, V. (2007). Cue exposure therapy for the treatment of opiate addiction: Results of a randomized controlled clinical trial. *Psychotherapy and Psychosomatics, 76,* 97–105.

Marissen, M., Franken, I., Blanken, P., van den Brink, W., & Hendriks, V. (2005). Cue exposure therapy for opiate dependent clients. *Journal of Substance Use, 10,* 97–105.

Marlatt, G. A. (2002). *Harm reduction: Pragmatic strategies for managing high-risk behaviors.* New York: Guilford.

Marsden, J., Gossop, M., Stewart, D., Best, D., Farrell, M., Lehmann, P., et al. (1998). The Maudsley Addiction Profile (MAP): A brief instrument for assessing treatment outcome. *Addiction, 93,* 1857–1867.

Martens, M. P., Pederson, E. R., LaBrie, J. W., Ferrier, A. G., & Cimini, M. D. (2007). Measuring alcohol-related protective behavioral strategies among college students: Further examination of the Protective Behavioral Strategies Scale. *Psychology of Addictive Behaviors, 21,* 307–315.

McConnaughy, E. A., Prochaska, J. O., & Velicer, W. F. (1983). Stages of change in psychotherapy: Measurement and sample profiles. *Psychotherapy: Theory, Research and Practice, 20,* 368–375.

Mercer, D. E., & Woody, G. E. (1999). *An individual drug counseling approach to treat cocaine addiction: The Collaborative Cocaine Treatment Study Model.* Washington, DC: National Institute on Drug Abuse. http://www.drugabuse.gov/TXManuals/IDCA/IDCA1.html

Miller, W. R., & Tonigan, J. S. (1997). Assessing drinkers' motivation for change: The stages of change readiness and treatment eagerness scale (SOCRATES). In G. A. Marlatt, & G. R. VandenBos (Eds.), *Addictive behaviors: Readings on etiology, prevention, and treatment* (pp. 355–369). Washington, DC: American Psychological Association.

Miller, W. R. (2000). Rediscovering fire: Small interventions, large effects. *Psychology of Addictive Behaviors, 14,* 6–18.

Miller, W. R., & Rollnick, S. (2002). *Motivational interviewing: Preparing people for change* (2nd ed.). New York: Guilford Press.

Montoya, I. D., & Vocci, F. (2008) Novel medications to treat addictive disorders. *Current Psychiatry Reports, 10,* 392–398.

Mosey, A. C. (1974). An alternative: the biopsychosocial model. *The American Journal of Occupational Therapy: Official Publication of the American Occupational Therapy Association, 28,* 137–140.

Nakawatase, T. V., Yamamoto, J., & Sasao, T. (1993). The association between fast-flushing response and alcohol use among Japanese Americans. *Journal of Studies on Alcohol, 54,* 48–53.

Nowinksi, J., & Baker, S. (1998). *The twelve-step facilitation handbook: A systematic approach to early recovery from alcoholism and addiction.* New York: Josey-Bass.

Nunes, E. V., & Levin, F. R. (2006). Treating depression in substance abusers. *Current Psychiatry Reports, 8,* 363–370.

Nutt, D., King, L. A., Saulsbury, W., & Blakemore, C. (2007). Development of a rational scale to assess the harm of drugs of potential misuse. *Lancet, 369,* 1047–1053.

Peele, S. (2000). What addiction is and is not: The impact of mistaken notions of addiction. *Addiction-Research, 8,* 599–607.

Petry, N. M., & Pietrzak, R. H. (2004). Comorbidity of substance use and gambling disorders. In H. R. Kranzler & J. A. Tinsley (Eds.), *Dual diagnosis and psychiatric treatment: Substance abuse and comorbid disorders.* (2nd ed., pp 437–459). New York: Marcel Dekker.

Pizzey, R., & Hunt, N. (2008). Distributing foil from needle and syringe programmes (NSPs) to promote transitions from heroin injecting to chasing: An evaluation. *Harm Reduction Journal, 5,* 24.

Prochaska, J. O., & DiClemente, C. C. (2005). The transtheoretical approach. In J. C. Norcross & M. R. Goldfried (Eds.), *Handbook of psychotherapy integration. (2nd ed.)* (pp. 147–171). New York, NY: Oxford University Press.

Project MATCH Research Group. (1997). Matching alcoholism treatments to client heterogeneity: Project MATCH post-treatment drinking outcomes. *Journal of Studies on Alcohol, 58,* 7–29.

Rawson, R. A., Gonzales, R., Marinelli-Casey, P., & Ang, A. (2007). Methamphetamine dependence: A closer look at treatment response and clinical characteristics associated with route of administration in outpatient treatment. *The American Journal on Addictions, 16,* 291–299.

Ries, R. K., Yuodelis-Flores, C., Comtois, K. A., Roy-Byrne, P. P., & Russo, J. E. (2008). Substance-induced suicidal admissions to an acute psychiatric service: Characteristics and outcomes. *Journal of Substance Abuse Treatment, 34,* 72–79.

Rogers, C. R. (1951). *Client-centered therapy; its current practice, implications, and theory.* Oxford, UK: Houghton Mifflin.

Rohsenow, D. J., Sirota, A. D., Martin, R. A., & Monti, P. M. (2004). The Cocaine Effects Questionnaire for patient populations: development and psychometric properties. *Addictive Behaviors, 29,* 537–553.

Rollnick, S., Heather, N., Gold, R., & Hall, W. (1992). Development of a short "readiness to change" questionnaire for use in brief, opportunistic interventions among excessive drinkers. *British Journal of Addiction, 87,* 743–754.

Rosenblum, A., Foote, J., Cleland, C., Magura, S., Mahmood, D., & Kosanke, N. (2005). Moderators of effects of motivational enhancements to cognitive behavioral therapy. *American Journal of Drug and Alcohol Abuse, 31,* 35–58.

Rotgers, F., Morgenstern, J., & Walters, S. T. (Eds.). (2006). *Treating substance abuse: Theory and technique* (2nd ed.). New York: Guilford Press.

Schroeder, J. R., & Moolchan, E. T. (2007). Ethnic differences among adolescents seeking smoking cessation treatment: A structural analysis of responses on the Fagerström Test for Nicotine Dependence. *Nicotine and Tobacco Research, 9,* 137–45.

Shane, A. P., Jasiukaitis, P., & Green, R. S. (2003). Treatment outcomes among adolescents with substance abuse problems: the relationship between comorbidities and post-treatment substance involvement. *Evaluation and Program Planning, 26,* 393–402.

Simmons, L. A., & Havens, J. R. (2007). Comorbid substance and mental disorders among rural Americans: Results from the National Comorbidity Survey. *Journal of Affective Disorders, 99,* 265–271.

Singhal, A., Tripathi, B. M., Pal, H. R., Jena, R., & Jain, R. (2007). Subjective effects of additional doses of buprenorphine in patients on buprenorphine maintenance. *Addictive Behaviors, 32,* 320–321.

Sitharthan, T., Sitharthan, G., Hough, M. J., & Kavanagh, D. J. (1997). Cue exposure in moderation drinking: A comparison with cognitive-behavior therapy. *Journal of Consulting and Clinical Psychology, 65,* 878–882.

Sloan, J. J., Bodapati, M., & Tucker, T. A. (2004). Respondent misreporting of drug use in self-reports: Social desirability and other correlates. *Journal of Drug Issues, 34,* 269–292.

Sobell, L. C., & Sobell, M. B. (1996). *Problem drinkers: Guided self-change treatment.* New York: Guilford.

Sobell, L. C., & Sobell, M. B. (1998). Guiding self-change. In W. R. Miller & N. Heather (Eds.), *Treating addictive behaviors* (pp. 189–202). New York: Plenum Press.

Sobell, L. C., & Sobell, M. B. (2000). Alcohol timeline follow-back. In American Psychiatric Association (Ed.), *Handbook of psychiatric measures.* Washington, DC: Author.

Sobell, L. C., & Sobell, M. B. (2005). Guiding self-change model of treatment for substance use disorders. *Journal of Cognitive Psychotherapy, 19,* 199–210.

Sobell, L. C., Ellingstad, T. P., & Sobell, M. B. (2000). Natural recovery from alcohol and drug problems: Methodological review of the research with suggestions for future directions. *Addiction, 95,* 749–764.

Sobell, L. C., Wagner, E., Sobell, M. B., Agrawal, S., & Ellingstad, T. P. (2006). Guided Self-Change: A brief motivational intervention for cannabis users. In R. Roffman & R. Stephen (Eds.), *Cannabis dependence: Its nature, consequences, and* treatment (pp. 204–224). Cambridge, UK: Cambridge University Press.

Stasiewicz, P. R., Vincent, P. C., Bradizza, C. M. , Connors, G. J., Maisto, S. A. & Mercer, N. D. (2008). Factors affecting agreement between severely mentally ill alcohol abusers' and collaterals' reports of alcohol and other substance abuse. *Psychology of Addictive Behaviors, 22,* 78–87.

Stockwell, T., Murphy, D., & Hodgson, R. (1983). The severity of alcohol dependence questionnaire: Its use, reliability and validity. *British Journal of Addiction, 78,* 145–155.

Tetrault, J. M., Desai, R. A., Becker, W. C., Fiellin, D. A., Concato, J., & Sullivan, L. E. (2008). Gender and non-medical use of prescription opioids: Results from a national US survey. *Addiction, 103,* 258–268.

Timko, C.,& DeBenedetti, A. (2007). A randomized controlled trial of intensive referral to 12-step self-help groups: One-year outcomes. *Drug and Alcohol Dependence, 90,* 270–279.

Tonigan, J. S., & Miller, W. R. (2002). The inventory of drug use consequences (InDUC): Test-retest stability and sensitivity to detect change. *Psychology of Addictive Behaviors, 16,* 165–168.

Trafton, J. A., Tracy, S. W., Olivia, E. M., & Humphreys, K. (2007). Different components of opioid-substitution treatment predict outcomes of patients with and without a parent with substance-use problems. *Journal of Studies on Alcohol and Drugs, 68,* 165–172.

Tryon, W. W., & Misurell, J. R. (2008). Dissonance induction and reduction: A possible principle and connectionist mechanism for why therapies are effective. *Clinical Psychology Review, 28,* 1297–1309.

Üstün, B., Compton, W., Mager, D., Babor, T., Baiyewu, O., Chatterji, S., et al. (1997). WHO Study on the reliability and validity of the alcohol and drug use disorder instruments: Overview of methods and results. *Drug and Alcohol Dependence, 47,* 161–169.

Walters, S. T., Rotgers, F., Saunders, B., Wilkinson, C., & Towers, T. (2003). Theoretical perspectives on motivation and addictive behavior. In F. Rotgers,J. Morgenstern, & S. T. Walters(Eds). *Treating substance abuse: Theory and technique (2nd ed.).* (pp. 279–297). New York, NY: Guilford Press.

Wampold, B. E., Mondin, G. W., Moody, M., Stich, F., Benson, K., & Ahn, H. (1997). A meta-analysis of outcome studies comparing bona fide psychotherapies: Empirically, "all must have prizes." *Psychological Bulletin, 122,* 203–215.

Warren, J., Stein, J. A., & Grella, C. E. (2007). Role of social support and self-efficacy in treatment outcomes among clients with co-occurring disorders. *Drug and Alcohol Dependence, 89,* 267–274.

Weiss, R. D., Griffin, M. L., Gallop, R. L., Najavits, L. M., Frank, A., Crits-Christoph, P., et al. (2005). The effect of 12-step self-help group attendance and participation on drug use outcomes among cocaine-dependent patients. *Drug and Alcohol Dependence, 77,* 177–184.

Weizenbaum, J. (1966). ELIZA – A computer program for the study of natural language communication between man and machine. *Communications of the Association for Computing Machinery, 9,* 36–135.

Westermeyer, J., & Thuras, P. (2005). Association of antisocial personality disorder and substance disorder morbidity in a clinical sample. *American Journal of Drug and Alcohol Abuse, 31,* 93–110.

Zacny, J. P., & Lichtor, S. A. (2008). Within-subject comparison of the psychopharmacological profiles of oral oxycodone and oral morphine in non-drug-abusing volunteers. *Psychopharmacology, 196,* 105–116.

Zvolensky, M. J., Feldner, M. T., Leen-Feldner, E. W., Gibson, L. E., Abrams, K., Gregor, K. (2005). Acute nicotine withdrawal symptoms and anxious responding to bodily sensations: A test of incremental predictive validity among young adult regular smokers. *Behavior Research and Therapy, 43,* 1683–1700.

7

Appendix

Inventory of Drug Use Consequences (InDUC-2L)

Instructions: Here are a number of events that people sometimes experience in relation to their use of alcohol and other drugs. Read each one carefully, and circle the number that indicates whether this has **ever** happened to you (0 = No, 1 = Yes). If an item does not apply to you, circle zero (0).

Has this **ever** happened to you? Circle one answer for each item.	No	Yes
1. I have had a hangover or felt bad after drinking or using drugs.	0	1
2. I have felt bad about myself because of my drinking or drug use.	0	1
3. I have missed days of work or school because of my drinking or drug use	0	1
4. My family or friends have worried or complained about my drinking or drug use.	0	1
5. I have enjoyed drinking or using drugs.	0	1
6. The quality of my work has suffered because of my drinking or drug use.	0	1
7. My ability to be a good parent has been harmed by my drinking or drug use.	0	1
8. After drinking or using drugs, I have had trouble with sleeping, staying asleep, or nightmares.	0	1
9. I have driven a motor vehicle while under the influence of alcohol or other drugs.	0	1
10. Drinking or using one drug has caused me to use other drugs more.	0	1
11. I have been sick and vomited after drinking or using drugs.	0	1
12. I have been unhappy because of my drinking or drug use.	0	1
13. Because of my drinking or drug use, I have lost weight or not eaten properly.	0	1

From: M. Earleywine: *Substance Use Problems*

Has this **ever** happened to you? Circle one answer for each item.	No	Yes
14. I have failed to do what is expected of me because of my drinking or drug use.	0	1
15. Drinking or using drugs has helped me relax.	0	1
16. I have felt guilty or ashamed because of my drinking or drug use.	0	1
17. While drinking or using drugs I have said or done embarrassing things.	0	1
18. While drinking or using drugs my personality has changed for the worse.	0	1
19. I have taken foolish risks when I have been drinking or using drugs.	0	1
20. I have gotten into trouble because of drinking or using drugs.	0	1
21. While drinking or using drugs, I have said harsh or cruel things to someone.	0	1
22. When drinking or using drugs, I have done impulsive things that I regretted later.	0	1
23. I have gotten into a physical fight while drinking or using drugs.	0	1
24. My physical health has been harmed by my drinking or drug use.	0	1
25. Drinking or using drugs has helped me to have a more positive outlook on life.	0	1
26. I have had money problems because of my drinking or drug use.	0	1
27. My marriage or love relationship has been harmed by my drinking or drug use.	0	1
28. I have smoked tobacco more when I am drinking or using drugs.	0	1
29. My physical appearance has been harmed by my drinking or drug use.	0	1
30. My family has been hurt by my drinking or drug use.	0	1
31. A friendship or close relationship has been damaged by my drinking or drug use.	0	1
32. I have spent time in jail or prison because of my drinking or drug use.	0	1
33. My sex life has suffered because of my drinking or drug use.	0	1
34. I have lost interest in activities and hobbies because of my drinking or drug use.	0	1

From: M. Earleywine: *Substance Use Problems*   © 2009 Hogrefe & Huber Publishers

Has this **ever** happened to you? Circle one answer for each item.	No	Yes
35. When drinking or using drugs, my social life has been more enjoyable.	0	1
36. My spiritual or moral life has been harmed by my drinking or drug use.	0	1
37. Because of my drinking or drug use, I have not had the kind of life that I want.	0	1
38. My drinking or drug use has gotten in the way of my growth as a person.	0	1
39. My drinking or drug use has damaged my social life, popularity, or reputation.	0	1
40. I have spent too much or lost a lot of money because of my drinking or drug use.	0	1
41. I have been arrested for driving under the influence of alcohol or other drugs.	0	1
42. I have been arrested for other offenses (besides driving under the influence) related to my drinking or other drug use.	0	1
43. I have lost a marriage or a close love relationship because of my drinking or drug use.	0	1
44. I have been suspended/fired from or left a job or school because of my drinking or drug use.	0	1
45. I have used drugs moderately, without having problems.	0	1
46. I have lost a friend because of my drinking or drug use.	0	1
47. I have had an accident while using or under the influence of alcohol or drugs.	0	1
48. While using or under the influence of alcohol or drugs, I have been physically hurt, injured, or burned.	0	1
49. While using or under the influence of alcohol of drugs, I have injured someone.	0	1
50. I have broken things or damaged property while using or under the influence of alcohol or drugs.	0	1

InDUC Scoring Sheet

Physical Items: 1, 8, 11, 13, 24, 29, 33, 48

Inter/Intra Personal Items: 4, 7, 17, 21, 27, 30, 31, 39, 43, 46

Impulse Personal Items: 2, 12, 16, 18, 34, 36, 37, 38

Social Control Items: 9, 10, 19, 22, 23, 28, 32, 41, 42, 47, 49, 50

Responsibility Items: 3, 6, 14, 20, 26, 40, 44

Control Scale Items: 5, 15, 25, 35, 45

Shortened Inventory of Problems – Alcohol and Drugs (SIP-AD)

Instructions: Here are a number of events that people sometimes experience in relation to their use of alcohol and other drugs. Read each one carefully, and circle the number that indicates whether this has **ever** happened to you (0 = No, 1 = Yes). If an item does not apply to you, circle zero (0).

Has this **ever** happened to you? Circle one answer for each item.	No	Yes
1. I have been unhappy because of my drinking or drug use.	0	1
2. Because of my drinking or drug use, I have lost weight or not eaten properly.	0	1
3. I have failed to do what is expected of me because of my drinking or drug use.	0	1
4. While drinking or using drugs my personality has changed for the worse.	0	1
5. I have taken foolish risks when I have been drinking or using drugs.	0	1
6. While drinking or using drugs, I have said harsh or cruel things to someone.	0	1
7. When drinking or using drugs, I have done impulsive things that I regretted later.	0	1
8. I have had money problems because of my drinking or drug use.	0	1
9. My physical appearance has been harmed by my drinking or drug use.	0	1
10. My family has been hurt by my drinking or drug use.	0	1
11. A friendship or close relationship has been damaged by my drinking or drug use.	0	1
12. I have lost interest in activities and hobbies because of my drinking or drug use.	0	1
13. My drinking or drug use has gotten in the way of my growth as a person.	0	1
14. My drinking or drug use has damaged my social life, popularity, or reputation.	0	1
15. I have spent too much or lost a lot of money because of my drinking or drug use.	0	1

From: M. Earleywine: *Substance Use Problems*

SIP-AD Scoring Sheet

Physical Items: 13, 29

Inter/Intra Personal Items: 21, 30, 31, 39

Impulse Personal Items: 12, 18, 34, 38

Social Control Items: 19, 22

Responsibility Items: 14, 26, 40

© 2009 Hogrefe & Huber Publishers